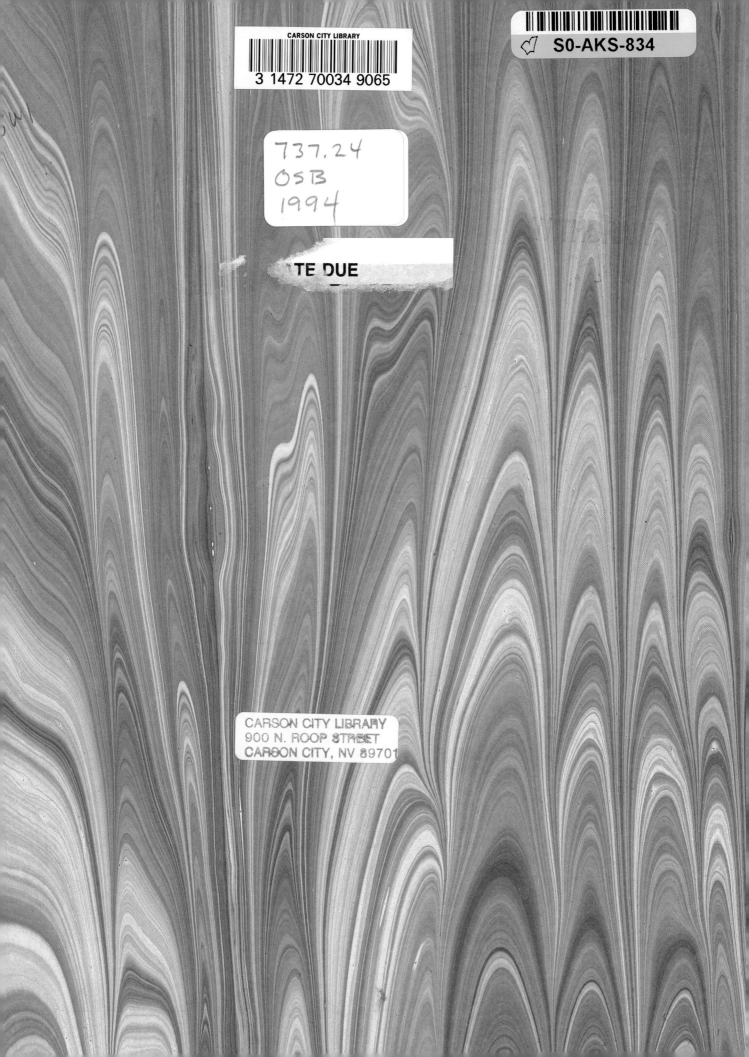

fun buttons

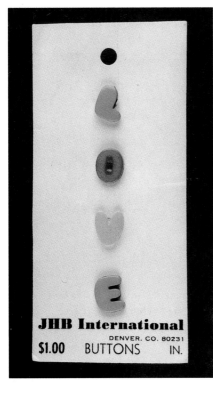

JHB International

DENVER, CO. 80231

$1.00   BUTTONS   IN.

WITH
PRICE GUIDE

Peggy Ann Osborne

Schiffer Publishing Ltd

77 Lower Valley Road, Atglen, PA 19310

ACKNOWLEDGMENTS

Pewter Chinaman in shackles,
reproduction of a nineteenth-century
French button, ca. 1970s.

My hands would have been tied without the help of many friends and associates. Thank you Mary Louise VandeBerg, Marion Roche, Claire Garrity, Laurel Brown Emmert, Colleen Farevaag, Judy Wehner, David Rector with Blue Moon Buttons, Debra Hill with Britex Fabrics, David Schoenfarber with Streamline Buttons, Pat Molnar with Buttons n Things and Druscilla White with Duttons for Buttons (England) for sending buttons to be photographed. And thank you M. W. (Freddie) Speights for your constant encouragement to me personally, as well as for sharing your extraordinary knowledge of the subject with all members of the button fraternity through the National Button Bulletin; it has been both a joy to read and a fount of information under your editorship.

And to Peter Schiffer, my publisher, and Nancy Schiffer, my editor, the acknowledgment that but for your advise, mentoring and aid, there would have been no books at all; but more importantly, that with your friendship, there is far more light in my world. Thank you.

Copyright © 1994 by Peggy Ann Osborne.
Library of Congress Catalog Card Number: 94-65981

All rights reserved. No part of this work may be reproduced or used in any forms or by any means — graphic, electronic or mechanical, including photocopying or information storage and retrieval systems — without written permission from the copyright holder.

Printed in Hong Kong.
ISBN: 0-88740-691-2

3174 3668 ✓

Published by Schiffer Publishing, Ltd.
77 Lower Valley Road
Atglen, PA 19310
Please write for a free catalog.
This book may be purchased from the publisher.
Please include $2.95 postage.
Try your bookstore first.

We are interested in hearing from authors
with book ideas on related subjects.

DEDICATION

For Marion Roche
my oldest button friend

and Rachel Wilson
my youngest button friend

Title page:
Snakeskin with brass initial, ca. 1950s.
Plastic realistic set, ca. 1990ss. 1/2" each.
Celluloid wafer button with ivoroid (imitation ivory made of celluloid), ca. 1920s.
Transfer on plastic, ca. 1986.

CONTENTS

Realistic heart, malachite, ca. 1980s.

Wolf of black horn inlaid with silver,
brass and tesserae, ca. 1880s.

FOREWORD

     This is not the first book published about buttons, but it is the first
one I have had fun with. Having put out 24 books myself, I know how hard it
is to keep the fun alive, yet Peg Osborne has done just that and snuck in the
facts as well. I have learned more about buttons from this charming book
than from all of my own books combined!

     The book highlights many of the materials used by button manufac-
turers, but more than that, it illuminates the myriad of subjects that the
designers have used over the years to tickle the public's fancy. Seeing them
pictured here has tickled mine!

     I dare you to read this book and not crack a smile or chuckle to
yourself. I couldn't do it. And it's all done with a flair for the unexpected and
the absurd.

     Illustrated with nearly 400 color photographs, Peg Osborne presents
the fun of buttons with examples of both the "once dear and rare" and the
"once everyday" with an equal respect. She finds their value (and shares it
with us) in their humor. Even I don't get that much respect!

     Her previous two books on buttons are respected classics in the
field, one as a best-selling identification guide and the other as a
much-heralded cultural history. But this one is the reflection of the lady
herself: fun. She sneaks up on you, teaching while amusing, and before you
know it, you have once again learned something!

     Before I met this lady, I knew only one thing about buttons. Well,
OK, I knew one other thing as well: there's always one that needs to be
sewed on somewhere on my shirts. Now, what don't I know!

     This book might just turn me into a collector--I'm having so much
fun I may stop looking *at* buttons and look *for* buttons instead.

Tom Wolfe

West Jefferson, N.C.

INTRODUCTION

Most button fanciers seem to fall into two camps: those who are fascinated by the materials buttons are made from and those who relish the designs on them. Materials of buttons made over the last 350 years range quite literally from A through Z. Their designs also are nearly endless and far more varied than a newcomer to the field would ever imagine. They run the gamut from silly to serious, from people to objects, from buildings and scenes to games and sports, and from animals to vegetables. I dare anyone to give me a subject for which there is not a button to match. I will win!

Most people become collectors by finding that a particular category of buttons relates to their other interests; a collector of desk paperweights might search for the tiny glass paperweight buttons, while a sailor would be more interested in buttons picturing boats. As people continue to collect, the range of subjects expands until they are hopelessly hooked on buttons!

A minority of collectors base their acquisitions on age rather than subject or material: there are those who specialize in only 'moderns' (in button parlance, modern refers to any button made since World War I ended in 1918) and a very few who limit their collecting (and wreck their budgets!) to eighteenth- century buttons.

Realistic head of inlaid Fimo clay, artist-made but commercially available, ca. 1992.

PART I BUTTON MATERIALS

Just in case anyone has already decided to challenge my assertion that an alphabet of materials has been used to make buttons, lets try it....

A: abalone, antler, agate, aluminum
B: bone, bamboo, Bakelite, brass
C: cork, celluloid, carnelian, cinnabar, coconut shell, coral
D: diamonds
E: enamels
F: fur, fabric
G: gold, glass
H: horn
I: ivory, iron
J: jet, jade, jewels
K: kidskin
L: leather, lithographs, Lucite
M: mother-of-pearl,
N: nuts, nylon
O: onyx
P: pewter, papier-mache, plastic, porcelain, pottery
Q: quartz
R: rhinestones, rock crystal
S: straw, silver, steel, snakeskin
T: tin, tombac, tortoise shell
U: under-glass (type of French button, usually 18th century)
V: vegetable ivory
W: wood
X:...Whoops! Coffee break! Be right back.....
Y: yarn
Z: zebrawood

Button materials can be divided into two major categories: those made from natural material and those from man-made materials.

1 NATURAL MATERIALS

Before the twentieth century, natural materials accounted for far more buttons of commercial manufacture than they do now. Mother-of-pearl buttons were made by the millions. Vegetable ivory button manufacture in South America was another huge industry. Horn, from the processed horns of cattle, was a very popular button material during the mid- to late nineteenth century, and even the bones of the cattle were used to make the plain underwear buttons worn by generations of men worldwide. Wood, ivory, tortoise shell, coconut shell, and assorted minerals and gemstones are among the other natural materials that button makers regularly employed.

MOTHER-OF-PEARL AND SHELL

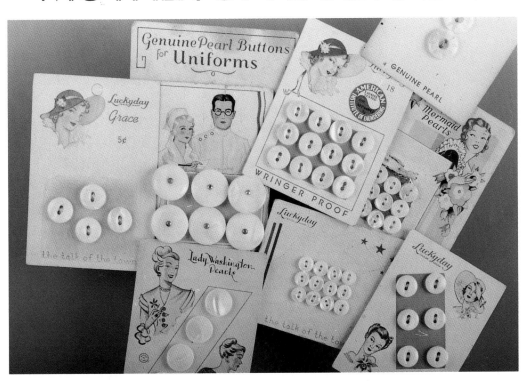

A great many people simply never think about buttons, unless one falls off their shirt! And when they do think of them it's those little round white shirt buttons that they consider. Depending on their age, the buttons in mind are plastic or pearl.

Mother-of-pearl was made into far more exciting buttons than that! The pearl buttons worn by men in the late-eighteenth century were often large and beautifully engraved, or set with paste gems. Ladies' clothing was often adorned with pearl buttons during the nineteenth century, and the variety of techniques used to decorate these pearls was astounding; many still survive, a testament to the sturdy permanence of this material. The pearl button industry died out in the twentieth century with the advent of hard plastics which were cheaper and less labor intensive to manufacture.

Mother-of-Pearl and shell buttons, 1870-1960, including from top left: helmet shell, pinna shell (very rare), cowrie, striped trocas , cowrie, pauwa, black shell, conch, white shell, iridescent olive, abalone, spotted, fresh water cat's-eye shell pearl (mollusk), and green snail. Sizes range from 1 2/3" to 1/2".

A rather unusual group of laminated, inlaid, and/or applied
pearl-on-pearl buttons. Several have faceted bits of cut steel riveted
on as additional trimming, ca. 1870s-1900. 1/2" to 2".

Mother-of-pearl buttons with decorations that were dyed, hand-painted, etched and/or gilded, ca. 1860-1910. 1/2" to 1 1/3"".

Opposite page:
Hand-painted Persian scenes in the same technique used for centuries in miniature paintings and illuminated books. The button seen at the upper right is painted on camel bone. All the rest are painted on mother-of-pearl, mounted in silver button frames. The large set is a rarity--most have long been broken up for individual sale. These are difficult to date, but it is known that most of them were exported from Iran during the late 1940s. Some may have been painted much earlier, but it is unlikely any have been made since.

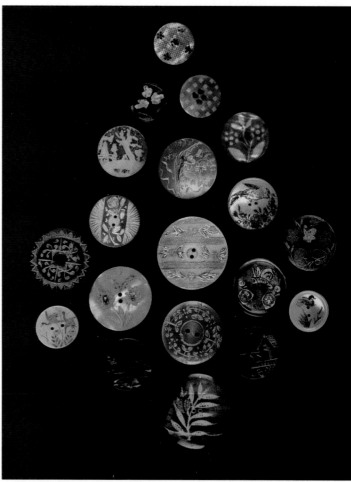

Mother-of-pearl buttons with transfer and/or stenciled designs. It is quite difficult to find the colored transfers in good condition and also rare to find them in the larger size, ca. 1865-1890. 1/2" to 1 1/4".

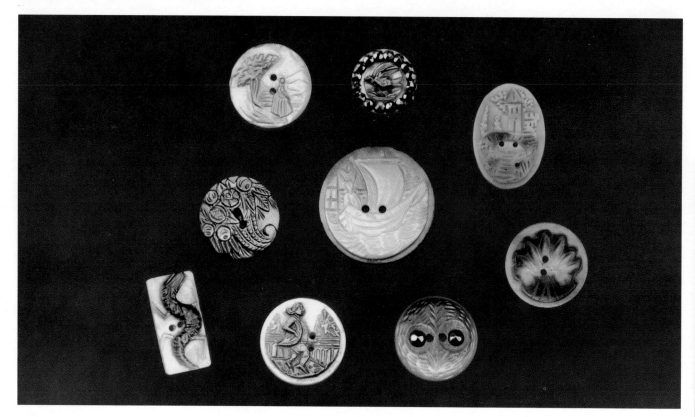

Cameos are among the most beautiful types of pearl buttons. Shell
was not commonly used for cameos earlier. Most of them date from
the late 30 years of the nineteenth century. The top center button is
rimmed with cut-steel facets that were individually rivited on, as
were the owl's eyes, lower right.

Mother-of-pearl with metal escutcheons, ca. 1890-1950. The shaded
pearl at center is the earliest and finest of the group. 1/2" to 1 1/2".

Mother-of-pearl realistics (buttons in the shape of the actual object represented). Almost all pearl realistics date from the twentieth century. The realistics on the corners of the page are dyed pearls ca. 1940-1950s. 1/3" to 1 1/3".

VEGETABLE IVORY

Vegetable ivory is the fruit of the tagua nut, from the Corozo palm trees in the rain forests of South America. Although most people today have never heard of it, vegetable ivory was once--from about 1870 to 1920--the most commonly-used material for manufactured buttons. Button companies began using it as an ivory substitute when they discovered that the cheap and plentiful nuts could be sliced, drilled, carved, dyed, and pressure molded.

The tagua nut is so closely grained that dyes can not penetrate beyond the first layer. Instead of a hindrance, the button makers used this to their advantage: when a dyed vegetable-ivory button was carved, a manufacturer automatically had a two-toned button--the carved areas remained white. Because button holes were always drilled after the dying and decorating stages, their inside walls also stayed white. Knowing this, collectors can differentiate vegetable -ivory buttons from others.

Vegetable-ivory buttons were very seldom large in size. The tagua nuts--each about the size of a golf ball--were peeled, then sliced into discs; only the center slice was over 1 1/2 inches in diameter. The vast majority of vegetable-ivory buttons are small.

Vegetable ivory buttons with fabric centers, steel and brass trim, pearl inlays, glass set-ins, molded tops, carved designs, and stenciled patterns. The large examples, although rather plain, are unusual. 3/ 8" to 1 1/2.

The top four buttons are unusual vegetable ivory realistics: a horseshoe, ladybug, door knocker (the ring actually does move) and jockey cap. The rarest example here is the button at the left with the inset glass intaglio dog's head. The button below it is engraved and the remaining four are decorated with metal escutcheons. 2/3" to 1".

Simple carvings highlight the two-toned effect of these vegetable ivories. They were first dyed, then tooled to expose the white color of the natural nut, giving them the appearance of a more complex decor. Manufacturers made much use of this effect. 1/3" to 4/5".

Compression molded pictorial designs, this group of vegetable ivories includes two military uniform buttons at the bottom. 1/3" to 1 1/2".

Vegetable ivory buttons with stenciled decor; these pictorial designs can be difficult to find. 2/3" to 1 1/8".

These two vegetable ivory buttons with hand-painted heads of Guatemalans are from the same period as those in the next photo but are far more unusual and of a higher quality of workmanship; outdoor scenes were the more common decor. 1 1/8".

Imports from Guatemala, ca. 1950. The top button was decorated with a transfer; the rest were hand-painted. The painted decor is fragile and peels easily--be careful with them if you are lucky enough to find one in good condition. 1" to 1 1/3".

From Japan, this very unusual hand-painted button is made from a thick slice of tagua nut, left unpeeled and in its natural contour. Although Japan continued to use vegetable ivory for jewelry and buttons long after the western world had quit doing so in favor of plastics, they were almost always plain buttons for men's suits and coats, ca. 1950s. 1 1/2".

IVORY

Ivory buttons from Japan, etched and painted. The Japanese used elephant tusk ivory, ca. 1920-1950. 2/3" to 1 1/4".

This Japanese button, a rose, was cameo-carved from ivory during the 1920-1950 period.

same as above

A scrimshawed ivory button etched and pigmented on an exceedingly thin disc of ivory; a rarity from the early-to-mid-nineteenth century.

Ivory realistics from Alaska. The Eskimos used tusk ivory from walruses, and, whenever they found it, fossilized ivory from the tusks of long-buried mammoths. Fossilized ivory has a very different mottled translucent and opaque look, as can be seen in the polar bear, ca. 1950s. 1".

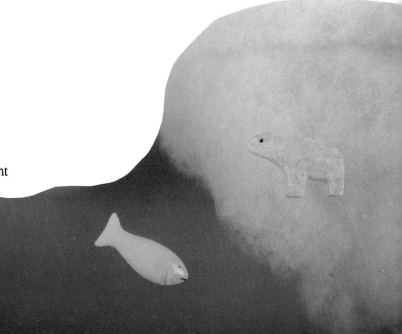

BONE

A very early realistically-shaped moth carved from bone. The great
majority of realistics, especially those made from bone, are far more
recent. This one was decorated with punched and chiseled details,
ca. mid-nineteenth century.

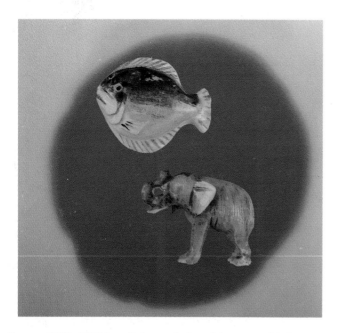

Recent (1930s-1950s) realistics made from bone, carved in Japan.
Although not particularly old or of any intrinsic value, these are now
hard to find and desirable buttons.

Opposite page:
Bone, usually from cattle, was one of the common button materials
of the past, but is seldom used now. The upper right button is a
1990 Tibetan import. Others include, at upper left, a carved Balu
tribe death mask from Africa; top center, a bone octagon overlaid
with a mosaic of mother-of-pearl; below it, a cameo-carved, dyed,
arts-and-crafts style button; to its left, a very old bone disc with a
pearl star escutcheon, and to its right, a scrimshaw. The three small
center buttons with black and white transfers are quite unusual, ca.
1860. Two of the buttons shown are topped with a thin layer of
tortoiseshell and several others have mother-of-pearl overlays. The
pierced square and the largest button at bottom were carved in
China. The oldest, now darkened with age, from the early eighteenth century, is the pin-shanked and brass-rimmed example at the
far right. 1/3" to 1 2/3".

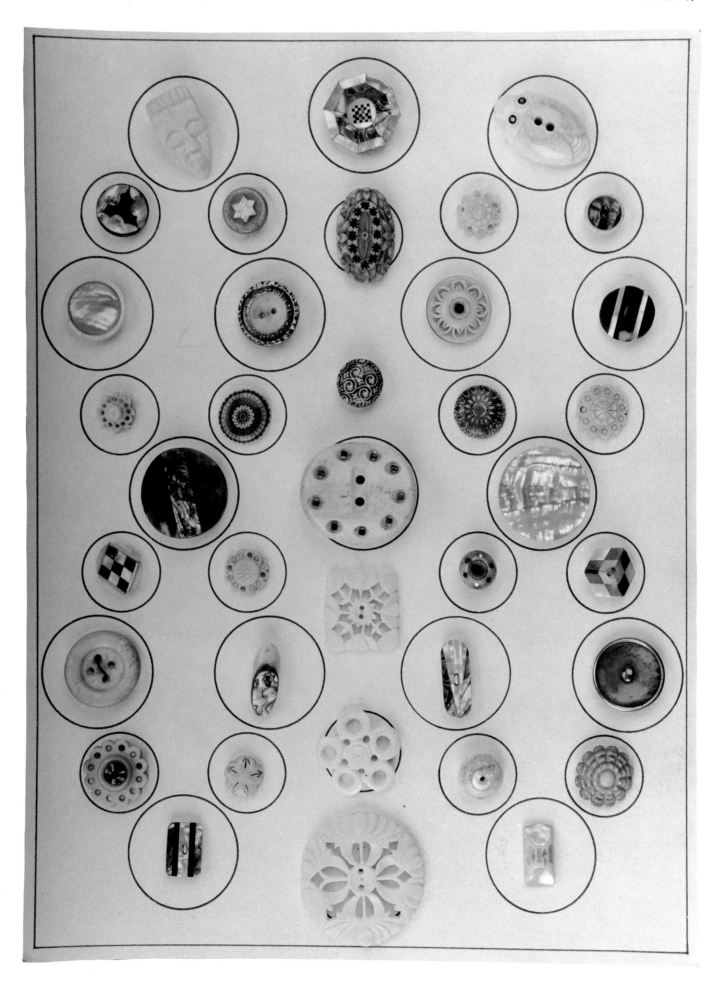

ANTLER

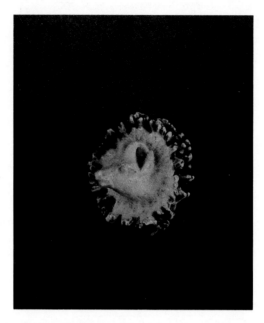

This deeply three-dimensional deer's head button was carved from a very different type of bone--natural antler. This is a rather high - quality example of the buttons carved in the Black Forest region of Germany during the last half of the nineteenth century. Popular as souvenirs for English Victorian travelers on the 'Grand Tour' of the continent, they were also worn locally on hunting jackets. The button has a silver loop-shank screwed into the reverse. 1 1/4".

Buttons of natural antler, assorted techniques, ca. 1910 and onward.

HORN

Pressure molded, dyed horn. The red, fluted-edged button was used on a hunter's coat, ca. mid-to-late 1800s.

Buttons made from animal horn, dyed black, ca. 1850-1890. Cattle were the main source, although buffalo horn was often used by American manufacturers. The pictured buttons include six with pearl inlays, two with pearl attachments, and one with cut-steel trim. 3/4" to 1 1/4".

A mounted collector's card of assorted horn buttons. Decorative techniques include basic carved details, etched designs, a gessoed and painted Chinese scene, and several inlays and overlays with pearl, tortoise shell, ivory, silver, and brass. Many of the buttons pictured are in the natural blonde color, and two are dyed black. There are also four red-dyed examples (the red oval features a compression-molded profile portrait of a youthful Queen Victoria), and two green-dyed buttons, at bottom and at far-right center. Red-dyed buttons are not nearly as often seen as natural or black horn; green examples are very few and far between. These range in age from the very beginning of the nineteenth century through the end.

COCONUT SHELL

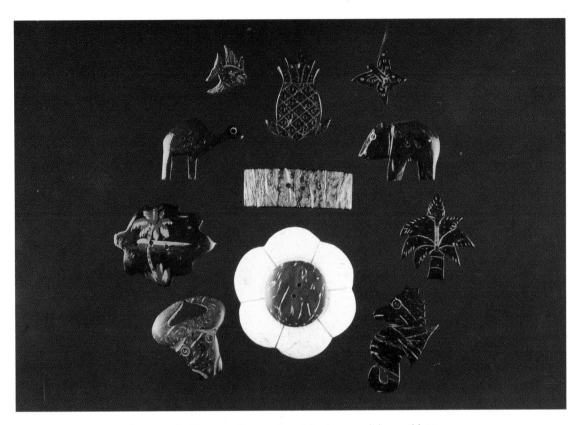

Coconut shell buttons from various islands around the world. Many of these were originally sold only as tourist souvenirs, but numbers of coconut shell buttons are now being imported by commercial button firms in Europe and the United States.

Painted coconut shell buttons made to imitate animal skins, reflecting the animal rights movement of the late twentieth century, ca. 1993.

Quite unusual but not at all practical for use, this button was made from the coir, or hair, covering a coconut.

WOOD

A large and lovely wooden button mounted in a brass rim and tinned-steel back from the middle of the nineteenth century. The portrait, which was pressure embossed onto the wood, is of Peter Paul Rubens, the Flemish painter of the late sixteenth and early seventeenth centuries. It was probably manufactured in celebration of the 300th anniversary of his birth in 1877. The Victorians greatly admired the zaftig ladies in his paintings, from which comes the term "having a rubenesque-like figure."

Assorted wooden buttons including hand-painted and stenciled designs, pressure embossed, *passementerie* (beaded), and carved examples. All are mid-twentieth-century buttons except for the two large pierced floral designs at the top of the photo, which date from the 1900-1920s. 3/4" to 1 1/2".

Original card of hand-painted wooden buttons from the 1950s.

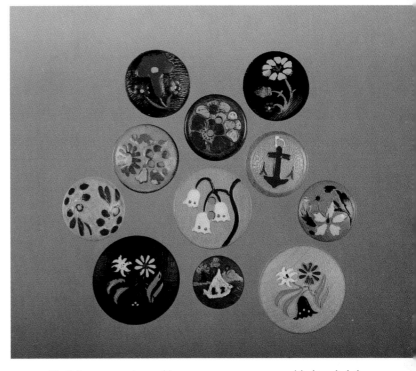

All of these natural wood buttons were pressure molded to slightly raise the pattern above the surface; they were then embellished with paint. Made in Czechoslovakia and Italy, ca. 1930s to 1950s.

These are hand-painted and pyrographed (a wood-burning technique) buttons from the U.S., France, Holland, and Czechoslovakia, ca. 1940s-1960s.

These highly varnished and uniquely three-dimensional wooden realistics came from Spain in the 1950s. They have metal loop-shanks on the reverse.

Wooden buttons from Czechoslovakia, 1930s. The top pair are toggled together with a heavy grosgrain ribbon, to fasten a sweater; the wood is covered in hand-painted paper imitating snake-skin. The bottom button has dyed wooden beads attached to it.

Wooden buttons trimmed with Bakelite, a popular combination during the 1930s.

Some unusual wooden realistics, including a carved and leather-handled purse at upper left, a rare Bakelite-trimmed mermaid, and a painted and yarn-strung blackboard button. On the bottom row, the door-knocker has a hanging plastic ring riveted on and the ladybug on the log is Bakelite, ca. 1930s-1940s.

A large, painted wooden button, a realistic cockatoo, ca. 1930s.

Dyed-wood realistics from the 1940s.

Painted realistics made from wood, ca. 1940s-1950s.

Burwood and Syrocco were both trade names of American manufactured, pressed-wood composition products made during the 1920s
and 30s. The wood was combined with other materials, made into a
pulp, and molded. They were usually sold in plain wood colors,
though some were dyed. The gold and silver-painted examples here

Each of these paisley designed buttons is made of metal, in a

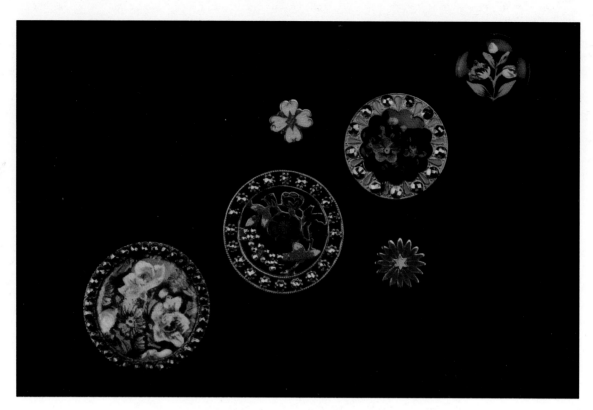

Assorted enameled buttons of the nineteenth century, including a
rare black emaux-peint, an unusual matte-finished pansy design at
lower left, a lovely pierced-brass with a riveted facet-cut steel border
and champlevé-enameled center flower, and the realistic yellow
baisse-taille dogwood blossom.

Modern enamel buttons on brass, in champlevé and cold enameling
techniques. Mostly from Japan, these were imported by JHB
International, the innovative American button firm, ca. 1980s.

This is a very specialized and rather deluxe collection of enamel buttons with rose designs. The enameling techniques are varied and include emaux-peints (painted enamels), cloisonné, champlevé, Limoges type, foil trimmed, and engine-turned baisse-taille. The oldest button seen here is the center oval, mounted in silver and dating to the very early nineteenth century. The rest range from the 1870s to 1910.

An assortment of twentieth -century buttons in brass, pewter, and white cast metal.

Aluminum buttons from the 1950s (center button) to the 1980s.

Many of the Norwegian pewter buttons manufactured during the 1960s and 1970s had typically Scandinavian scenes on them, such as cold weather animals and Viking ships, but the majority had snowflake designs as seen here.

Pewter buttons with elk, reindeer and polar bear designs. Buttons like these, often backmarked *'Norge'*, or Norway, were first seen on ski sweaters in shops in the United States in the 1960s. Before long, they were being imported for sale in yarn shops and enjoyed quite a fad for a number of years.

Modern pewter buttons from Battersea Buttons late in the 1970s and a current button, a realistic lion, from Danforth Pewterers. These are all backmarked with the company names. The Battersea buttons are also dated on the backs.

Metal has been the material most commonly used for satirical or somewhat scandalous button designs over the years. These two Victorian brass picture buttons have something in common, or maybe a lack of something...

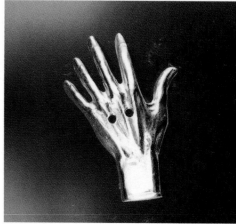

Sterling silver, hand-shaped button, ca. 1993. This button is great fun: the palm side is as detailed as is this side so that the buttons can be sewn on either way, giving a very different look to the outfit.

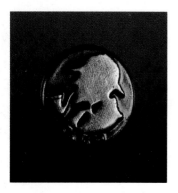

Modern button made of copper, picturing the great Sherlock Holmes himself, ca. 1950s-1960s.

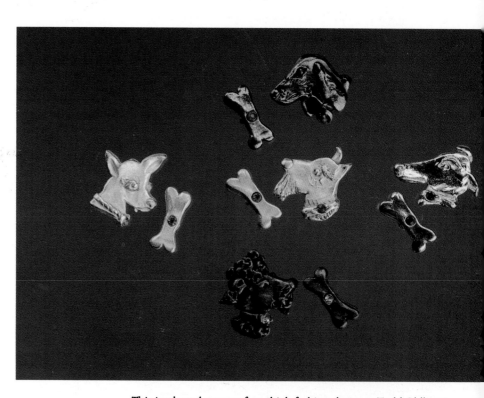

This is a brand new set from high fashion designer Todd Oldham's exclusive line of buttons, ca. 1993. The dogs--each done in a separate type of metal--have their own matching bones!

Another of the same type of rare French satirical sporting buttons shown at right, but from a different set. This one shows a fly fisherman holding his hand to his bottom, and the words "that bit!". Has he snagged part of his own anatomy instead of a fish?

A very rare and desirable set of satirical French hunt-theme buttons, in silver plate and brass. These show the hunter in various sorry states, including: 1) being knocked off his horse by a tree limb while crying "stop!", 2) trying to point out the rabbit to his seemingly unobservant dog, 3) yelling "not so fast" while trying to keep up with the fleeing rabbit and dog, and 4) in tears, sobbing "poor beast" after he has shot his own dog!

A modern aluminum button from Germany picturing a bear having treed a hunter. The tree is breaking so the hunter is in a rather frantic position, ca. 1950s-1960s!

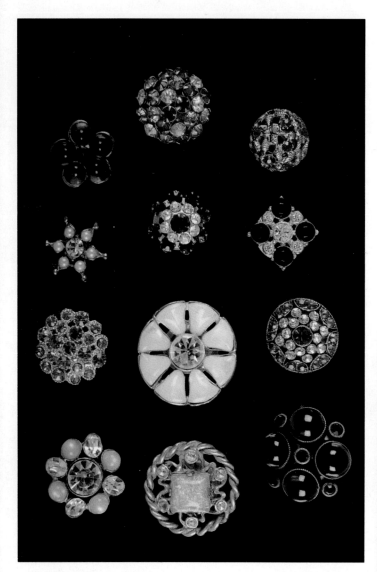

During the 1930s and again in the 1950s, this sort of jeweled button was the height of glamour. These are metal buttons with cup-set colored glass stones.

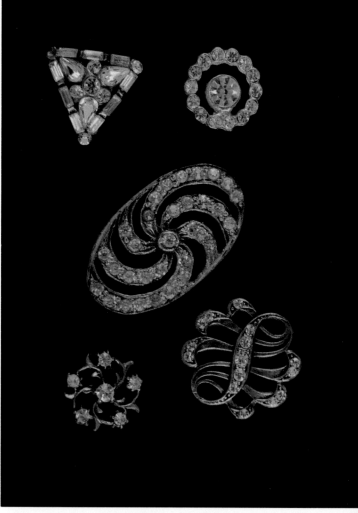

A few fine quality examples of prong-set rhinestone and metal buttons from the 1950s.

Known as "jelly-bellys", these are now quite collectible in brooch
form: the buttons are actually far rarer. Brass, set with glass stones,
ca. 1950s.

GLASS

An assortment of glass buttons dating from the mid-nineteenth
century through 1920 (the large flower). Top row: a very rare
example of passementerie red glass (individual tiny glass beads
hand- riveted to a metal frame), and a very dimensional, solid
rectangle of crackled glass. 2nd row: Camphor-glass with a
colored transfer design, milk-glass with a mother-of-pearl escutcheon center, and a molded glass button with an imitation-wood
finish. 3rd row: An extremely rare type of glass button with a ribbon
laid into pre-molded grooves and tied on the back, and milk glass
with a transfer design. Bottom, a huge flower in a satin-glass
finish.

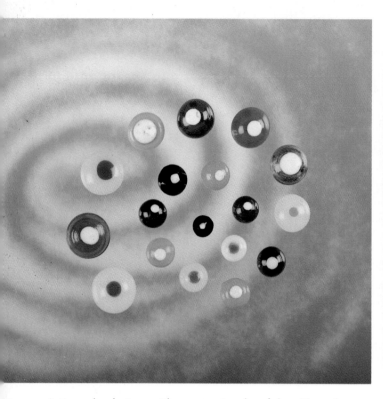

Antique glass buttons with a contrasting dot of glass. These date from the 1840-1850s period and were exported worldwide from the glassmaking areas of Silesia-Bohemia. They were worn on ladies' dresses, and children's clothing.

These lovely buttons are called 'precision-glass inlays' and that describes them rather well: a precisely cut piece of flashed (coated on the back to gleam) glass was glued into place in a pre-molded depression atop a glass button. They date from between the World Wars, though some were imported to the United States in the 1950s.

These glass buttons known as 'mirrors' date to the mid-nineteenth century. The larger ones are far more unusual, but it is not easy to find any mirror buttons of this age in good condition. They are backed with large metal plates with a loop shank attached.

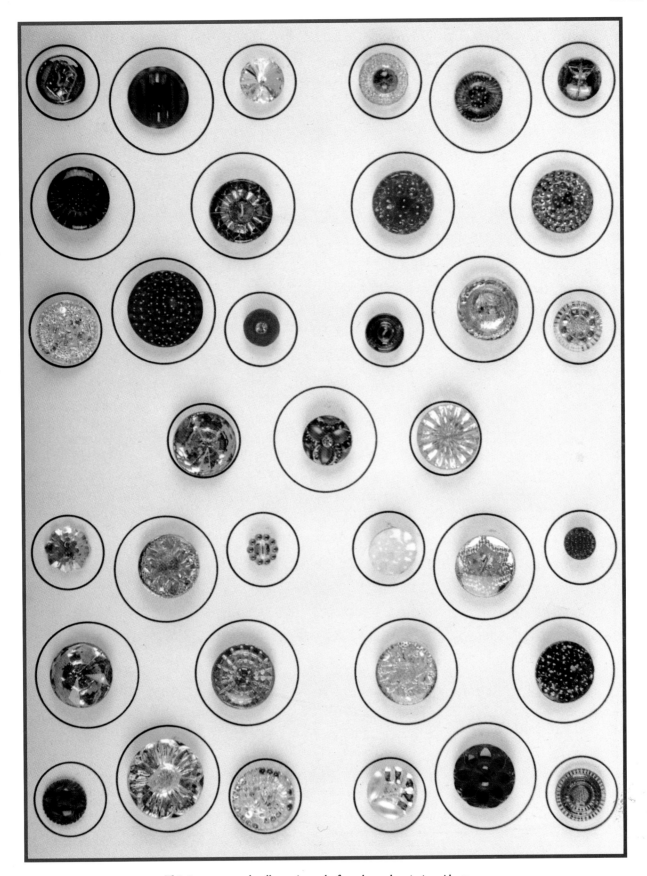

This is a mounted collector's card of modern glass 'mirror' buttons. Unlike the antique examples at left, these have painted backs, much like a wall-mirror has, instead of metal backs. They were made in Czechoslovakia between World Wars I and II (1920-1940). A few of the larger ones seen here were brought back from Russia in 1980 and had been made in (then) East Germany after World War II.

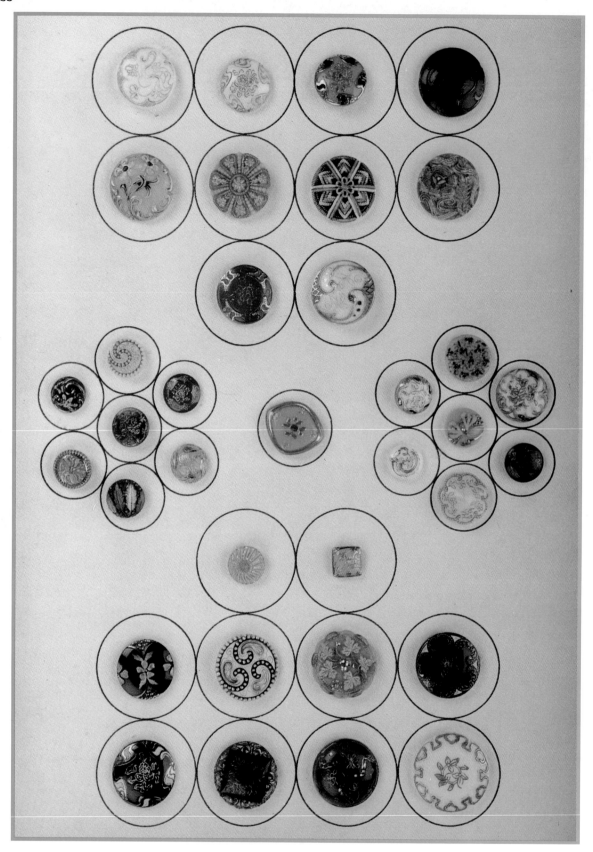

Collectors often refer to these as 'Victorian glass' buttons, a name
which leaves out the myriad of other types of glass buttons made
during that long era, but which does accurately date them to the last
half of the nineteenth century. They are molded, often in a slightly
domed shape, and with line designs of great variety. The designs are
accented with paints and/or lustres. This sort of button commonly
has a metal four-way box-shank inserted into the glass on the back.

West German molded and lustre-trimmed glass buttons from the
1950s.

These are fused and di-chromatic glass buttons made by two
different American glass artisans, ca. 1990. *Courtesy of Blue Moon
Button Art*

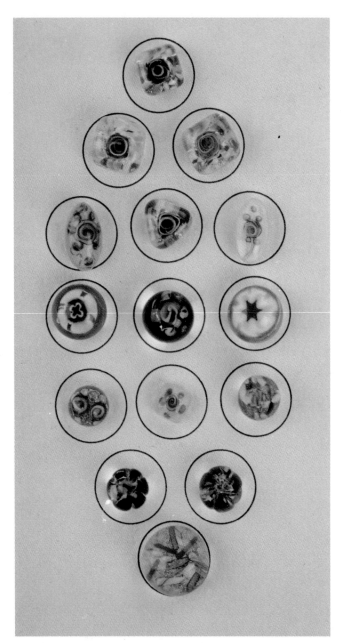

This paperweight button with the turtle design, and the four extraordinary examples below were made in 1993 by glass artist Will Stokes. His set-ups are both creative and technically complex, as can be seen in the spider paperweight button at the bottom complete with a three-dimensional, iridescent glass web and egg case underneath (which only can be seen from a side view through the highly domed button).

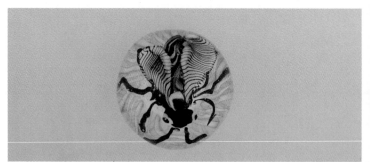

Paperweight buttons are a great favorite of many collectors. They are made exactly as are the larger and more known desk-sized glass paperweights but have a metal-loop shank inserted in the back while the glass is still molten. Artisans makes them by combining, over a heated torch, a glass base and an interior decoration (called the set-up), and enclosing it all within a clear cap of crystal. The heat fuses all of the parts into one seamless, solid mass. Paperweights are often called blown glass but this is patently wrong: paperweights are not blown but assembled. The paperweight buttons shown mounted on a card in this photo were all made between 1940 and 1990 and came from glassworkers in Czechoslovakia, France, and the United States.

Modern glass buttons, ca. 1930s, from Czechoslovakia. These have
often erroneously been called two-piece paperweights, but there is
no such thing. A paperweight, by definition, is one solid piece of
glass once it has been completed. These were made in two pieces,
with painted centers, and were glued --not fused -- together.

BLACKGLASS

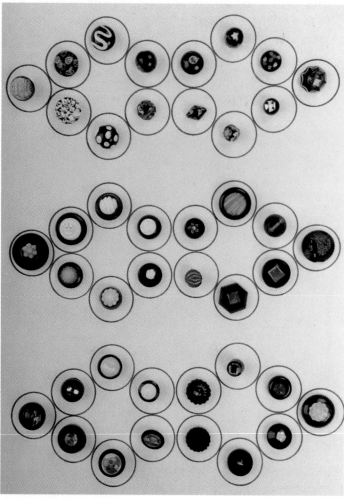

Black glass was a huge industry in the nineteenth century and buttons of this material were made by the millions, mostly in Europe. This is a mounted collector's grouping of assorted black-glass women's buttons in a variety of decorative technique, including buttons decorated with colored glass overlaid and fused and others with glass attached by more mechanical methods. The rest of the buttons shown are the inlays and the paperweights.

Black-glass buttons from the last decades of the nineteenth century decorated with molded details and coated in various lustred finishes.

FABRICS

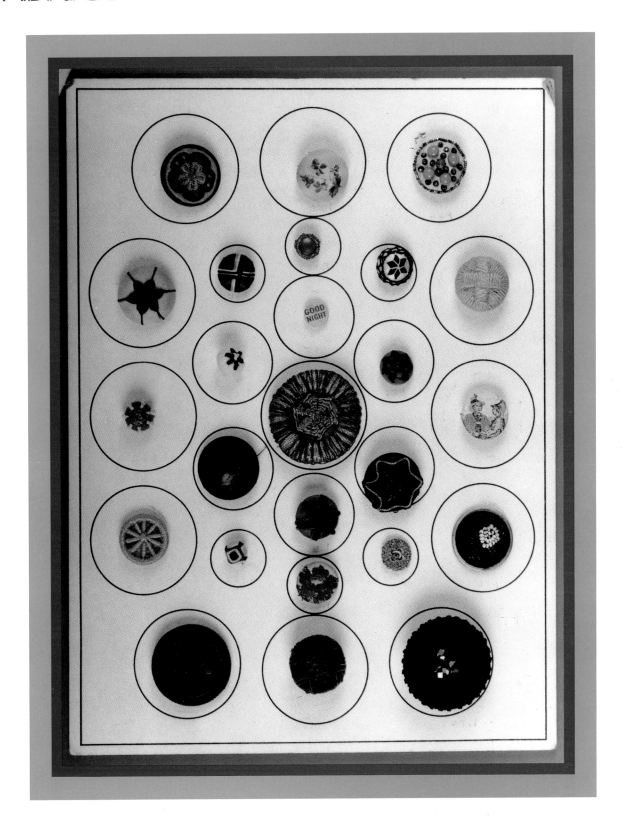

A mounted collection of fabric buttons from the nineteenth and
early twentieth centuries. Included are embroidered, woven silk,
passementerie trimmed and beaded examples.

PLASTICS

CELLULOID

Celluloid buttons, assorted techniques, dating from the late 1880s
(the five at far left) to the 1930s.

Very unusual and rather ludicrous in appearance. A celluloid wafer button with a Syrocco like molded wood escutcheon, ca. 1920s.

Celluloid buttons, ca. 1920s.

Two celluloid buttons: an imitation sew-through button with brass thread holes, and one imitating carved vegetable ivory.

An unusual type of celluloid button with a scene lithographed directly on it. It dates from the 1890s.

This is one of the most beautiful celluloid buttons, and one of the largest. It has three shanks on the reverse to steady it on clothing and was used as the single button atop an evening cape in the 1890s. The peacock was lithographed onto the celluloid in full color and decorated with inlaid vari-colored glass jewels. Very rare.

A solid and heavy celluloid wafer with a brass escutcheon in the Egyptian style of the 1890-1900 period, pre-dating the King Tut craze by a couple of decades, is another very deluxe button.

A brass-trimmed celluloid wafer button with small steel rivets holding the lady's head in place, 1890s.

A very sturdy openwork molded celluloid button reflecting the then-current Oriental mania, ca. 1920s.

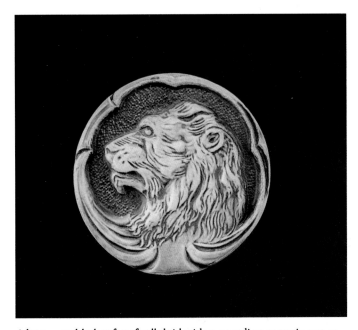

A heavy, molded wafer of celluloid with a great lion portrait, not an easy type to find, ca. 1920s-1930s.

The spectrum of colors common to Celluloid buttons, ca. 1910-1935.

A mounted collector's card of extruded celluloid buttons, ca. 1918-1940s. The celluloid strings, ribbons, and ropes, were formed by passing hot celluloid through tubes and pressing it out in long threads, much like a spaghetti-making machine would do. Once the threads were formed, they were tied in knots, wound in circles, or folded, as seen in the buttons pictured.

These are layered and laminated celluloid buttons, not such an easy type to find. The individual colors were formed as discussed in the last caption, but were then flattened and joined, ca. 1920s.

Although these are similar in appearance to the heavy solid-molded Bakelite buttons of the same era, these are celluloid. Bakelite was starting to displace celluloid and these were undoubtedly imitations of the newly popular material, offered by enterprising celluloid manufacturers. The designs reflect the chunky Machine Art style popularized in the late Cubism era by artists like Fernand Leger, ca. 1920 to 1930s.

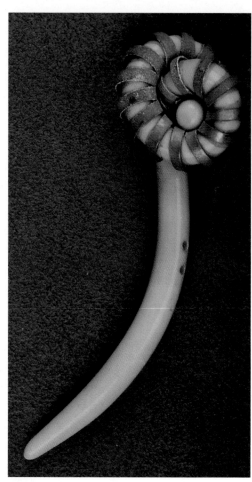

Another very odd celluloid button, quite large and trimmed in chrome, ca. 1920s.

Celluloid buttons in a variety of fun, realistically-shaped designs. The large clock face, though cheaply made and far too lightweight to be a really useful button, is very rare. The exotic bloom to its lower left is a deluxe celluloid button made for a designer. These are ca. 1920 to 1930s.

Celluloid realistics, ca. 1930s and 1940s.

BAKELITE

Assorted Bakelite buttons from the 1920s to 1940s, including a rare
laminated red, clear, and brown example at upper middle.

This is a laminated Bakelite button, the hardest type of Bakelite button to find. This one combines imitation-tortoiseshell colored layers with opaque brown and, although not very showy, is nevertheless quite attractive and very rare.

These appear similar to Lucite, yet they are Bakelite. Unlike Lucite, transparent Bakelite yellows with age. The top button had an actual butterfly pressed into it from the back while it was still warm from the manufacturing process. The bottom button was engraved on the back and then painted. The remaining buttons are laminated opaque and clear Bakelite combinations--which are easier to find than the type of laminated buttons seen in the last two photos, ca. 1930 to 1940s.

Bakelite was most often combined with wood (see examples under wooden buttons) or metal. These are ladies' Bakelite coat buttons with metal trim from the 1920s and early 1930s. The pictorials are hard to find.

All of these are Bakelite realistics. The glass-eyed animal heads,
upper right, are very rare and expensive. The butterfly, cat's head,
seahorse, and fish are also quite unusual and highly desirable, but
no Bakelite realistic is now ignored by collectors!

LUCITE

Clear Lucite button with a floral design carved and painted from the
back before the entire reverse was coated with a pearlized paint
finish, ca. 1950s.

Opposite page:
A collection of Lucite buttons from the 1950s. Techniques included
back carvings, laminations, various inlays, and metal, pearl, and
enamel trims.

HARD PLASTICS

An extraordinary and early hard-plastic button dating to before World War II. The unusual lacy rope border is made in very much the fashion of extruded celluloid. The center portion is plastic but with a glass dome featuring an under-glass, reverse painting of a pair of lovebirds.

These are called Artid buttons and were made in England during the 1950s. There were many different designs and are unique enough to make a great subspecialty for collectors of plastic buttons. The top two buttons pictured are Indian in inspiration and feature an aristocratic couple at left and the Hindu God, Lord Krishna, piping his flute, at right.

A group of molded plastic buttons from the 1930s and 1940s. These were all made by the Diamond Plastic Company and are always coated with a pearlized, metallic, or electro-plated finish, and backmarked with the company logo and patent numbers. The buttons from this company featured some the most creative and intriguing designs seen in plastic buttons, including the drunk with the Keystone Cop, and the surrealistic bar scene at lower right.

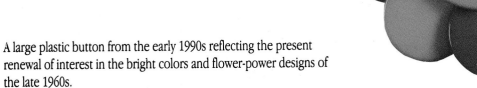

A large plastic button from the early 1990s reflecting the present renewal of interest in the bright colors and flower-power designs of the late 1960s.

A wonderfully varied group of plastic buttons mounted on a
collector's card. The techniques include inlays, overlays, assorted
materials as trim, electro-plated, laminated, and wood-finished

Imitations of tortoiseshell buttons were made in glass and Bakelite as well as the later hard plastics. This collection combines plastic and Bakelite examples. They were worn on ladies' overcoats in the 1930s and 1940s.

Since the extraordinary renaissance in button popularity that took place in the late 1980s around the world, manufacturers have supplied some wonderfully creative plastic buttons. The deer on this very high quality button from Germany was actually hand-cut and etched and is as sharp as glass, ca. 1990.

These plastic buttons were made in Germany in the early 1990s. The top left was designed to appeal to the Southwestern trend in the decorative arts. The one below it was made in reaction to the Neo-Geo decorative arts fad with its faux marble look and riveted strip of Roman numerals.

A pair of perfectly adorable plastic buttons from Germany. A sense of humor has returned to button design since a button boom began again in earnest during the mid-1980s, ca. 1993.

A pearlized finish in orange sets off the expressionistic Oriental design on this plastic button from 1991.

Plastic buttons from Japan, Germany, and the United States, ca.
1990. The realistic marten's head with glass eyes was made in
reactive support of the animal rights/anti-fur campaigns, it satirizes
the marten fur stoles of the 1930s and 1940s that featured heads
and paws dangling from them. The most recognizable button here
is a large realistic head of one of the cartoon Mutant Teenage Ninja
Turtles, part of a seet of four that came in two sizes from the
American company, Streamline Buttons.

One of the world's most successful novelty button companies, JHB
International, in the United States, sold these very bright and fun
hard plastic realistics late in the 1980s.

II BUTTON THEMES

There are subjects for button designs that are closer to the hearts of collectors than others. Perennial favorites include birds, flowers, cats (as well as all other animals), Oriental scenes, and buttons picturing beautiful women. Some collectors delight in the rarer subjects, the unexpected, and the unique. Following is a lighthearted look at buttons by theme:

The Good, the Bad, and the Ugly!

The devil, you say! Molded and electro-plated plastic button, ca. 1930s.

Ceramic angel button, hand-made and painted, U.S.A., ca. 1993.

Copper button with a perfectly ugly mythological beast, ca. 1900.

CLOTHING FASTENERS & ACCESSORIES

It is humorous to find other types of fasteners pictured on buttons, yet such designs have been used off and on since the eighteenth century.

It is amazing that button designers chose to picture buttons on buttons and even buckles on buttons, which were even more common. There are literally dozens of examples from the Victorian era alone, including the four shown here on the bottom row. The rest of the pictured buttons, except for the earlier bow at top left, are from the early to mid- twentieth century and include celluloid, fabric, and glass. The largest is a wonderfully tongue-in-cheek heavy plastic example from Germany, ca. 1990, with a large brass zipper pull attached only at the top so that it dangles freely. The idea of 'unzipping' a button is intriguing!

All of milady's (and milord's) accessories have been pictured on buttons.

Painted celluloid hat from the 1930s.

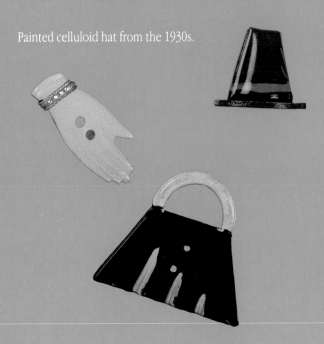

Left, umbrellas pictured on a tinted brass button, and right, a one-piece blackened and engraved brass button with a silver-plated hat attached, both ca. 1890s.

Celluloid buttons from the 1930s.

Two modern realistic shoes: left, a glass button from the 1930s, and right, plastic from the 1940s.

A specialized and fun grouping of Mexican hat buttons, from the 1930s and 1940s, including wood, ceramic and felt with beaded trim.

Objects have been no object to the button industry: buttons have pictured any and all!

This assortment of buttons includes (from top row) a plastic watermelon slice, brass and rhinestone flowerpot, celluloid parasol, Bakelite cheerleaders' bullhorn, brass safety pins, carved and painted Bakelite Japanese lantern (rare), sterling silver fan, ceramic dollar bill, plastic mitten, brass plated money bag, and brass wedding certificate, ca. 1930-1980.

Including part of the kitchen sink, literally any possible object was the subject of a button at one time or another--here are the water faucets, heavy cast metal realistics in chrome and brass plate, ca. 1993.

Actual coins have been turned into buttons in countries the world over for at least 200 years, but those shown here were always buttons and never real forms of money. These represent American, English, Mexican, French, and Greek coins, ca. 1930-1970.

Mother-of-pearl dagger, ca. 1940s.

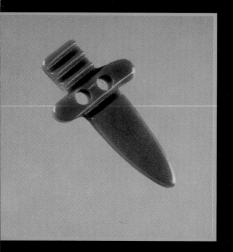

Bakelite dagger, ca. 1930s.

Weaponry seems an odd subject for buttons. Nevertheless, this, too, has been included in the pantheon of button designs over the years. Here are (clockwise from top) an enameled-brass pistol from the 1950s, a tinted-brass ball on a chain from the late 1800s, a Victorian button in brass and tin showing a hand grasping a dagger, a Bakelite handgun from the 1930s, and a brass dagger on-mother-of-pearl and mounted brass.

OCCUPATIONS

Each manufacturer tried to make their buttons more appealing to consumers.

Plastic candies, very rare, and very realistic buttons. Can you imagine the fun of wearing these buttons on your best spring coat? *Courtesy of Laurel Brown Emmert.*

Bakelite ice-cream cone button, metal-loop shank on back, ca, 1930s.

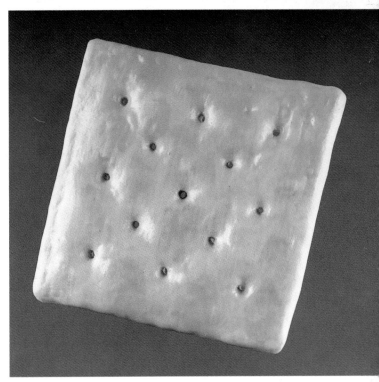

Soda-cracker realistic made of porcelain during the late 1980s by Stella Rzanski who has made many wonderful buttons specifically for collectors; this button, was, however, purchased at a retail fabric shop.

Not yet content, button manufacturers got the Butcher, the Baker, and even the Candlestick Maker in on the act!

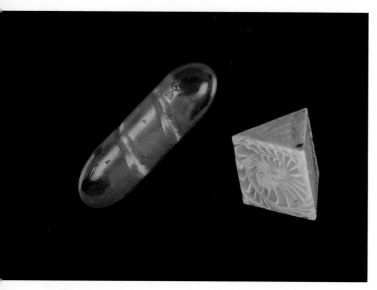

Sausage and cheese, Milwaukee's second-finest products! Celluloid realistics, ca. 1920-1930s.

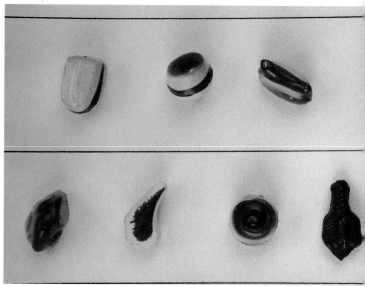

These two sets of realistics are now very rare: sandwiches and a butcher shop selection which date from the 1930s button craze.

From Japan, 1993, hard-plastic buttons showing the most American symbols of all, the hot dog and hamburger.

Breads & rolls, and slice of pie;
2 rare celluloid sets of the 1930s.

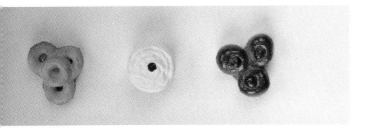

The Butcher Shop set and some of the set known as Deli Sandwiches: rare celluloid realistic buttons designed by Marion Weeber,
for B. Blumenthal Button Co, ca. 1940s.

Very rare, each of these humorous but quite deluxe realistic buttons
from the 1930s-1940s was hand assembled from six variously-tooled
pieces of celluloid.

Rich Men, Poor Men, Beggars and Thieves; Pirates, Clowns, and Indian Chiefs.

Wooden, hand-carved and painted, realistic pirate with brass earring, ca. early 1950s.

Novelty set, transfers on plastic, from one of America's more innovative button companies, JHB International, in the 1980s.

Plastic Indian-chief button, ca. 1950s.

Realistic clown, hard to find, an early plastic button, ca. 1930s.

Two versions of Native Americans in full headdress: right, pressed pewter, ca. 1920s; left, wood with paint trim and attached celluloid face, 1930s.

Bakelite realistic clown's head, very rare, ca. 1930s.

The Sheriff, a Knight, and even The Bard complete.

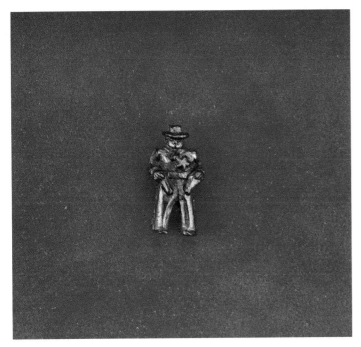

Brass realistic, rare. A sheriff with gun and badge, ca. 1930s.

Carved ivory realistic Roman soldier wearing a helmet, ca. 1950s.
Courtesy of Judy Wehner

Large molded celluloid coat button featuring William Shakespeare's likeness.

THE ARTS AND ENTERTAINMENT

Button makers had a ball with masks!

Brass button of a Greek lady holding a mask, ca. 1900.

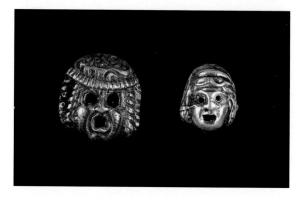

Two very early silver buttons, origin unknown, but not European or American. They may be eighteenth-century examples.

Plastic masks of drama's Comedy and Tragedy, ca. 1940s. The left button is electroplated.

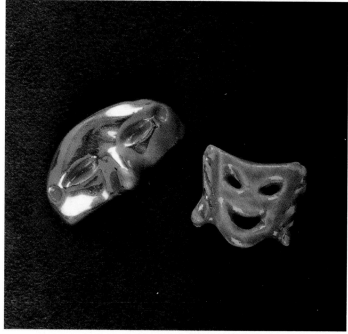

Two ceramic realistic drama masks, post-1950.

A glazed porcelain mask made for button collectors, late 1980s.

Carved-ivory set of the Japanese gods seen in the Noh Dramas. There are exact copies of this set in plastic from the same era, the 1950s.

Grotesquely humorous mask; a brass button from Japan, ca. 1950.

Carved cinnabar (a type of lacquer from the Orient) mask of a demon, from China. Realistically-shaped cinnabar buttons are very rare, ca. 1920s.

Plastic realistic, a South Seas Island style of mask, from the days of the *Kon Tiki* expedition.

From Sri Lanka, this button represents the mask of a demon. Painted papier mâche, with a metal-loop shank in the back, ca. 1980s.

A humorous Mexican button, heavy silver, with a dangling nose ring, ca. 1940s.

These buttons are from Peru. All are sterling silver except for the very heavy cast brass one in the center. The masks are those of Aztec gods; the one at the top is their Jaguar god, ca. 1950s.

African carved-wood mask button.

From Mexico in the early 1950s, copper mask buttons with soldered brass and copper features.

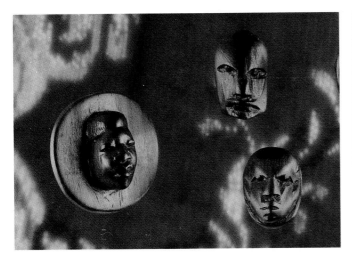

Carved wooden buttons from Kenya, ca. 1950s.

Kenyan carved-wood realistic.

Very stylized brass mask button from Africa, ca. late 1980s.

Another highly stylized mask design; carved horn button from Africa, ca. 1992.

Bakelite realistic African mask with metal earrings and paint trim, ca. 1930s.

Art and Music

Palettes seen on buttons. The artist seen on the funny pewter button (upper left) is holding his palette as a shield and wielding his large paintbrush as a sword. Below him are nineteenth-century, silver-lustred black-glass buttons, one with a hand on the palette and two of brass, including a modern one with painted trim. In the center, a painted-wooden button of the 1950s. Another brass one from the nineteenth century shows the artist Cellini and his tools. The two to the right and below are of porcelain and date from the 1980s. At the top right, three metal buttons are shown.—The first enameled, ca. 1980s, and two silver-plated from the 1800s. The pink and black painted and glitter-trimmed wooden palettes seen in the background are huge sew-through buttons from 1990.

Music themed buttons from the 1950s, in brass, plastic, glass, and wood.

Buttons showing musical instruments have been made since the late 1700s; these examples are all from the 1940s-1980s. Materials include ceramic, celluloid, white metal, brass, glass, and pewter.

CHILDREN

When button manufacturers ran out of ideas, they went back to School.

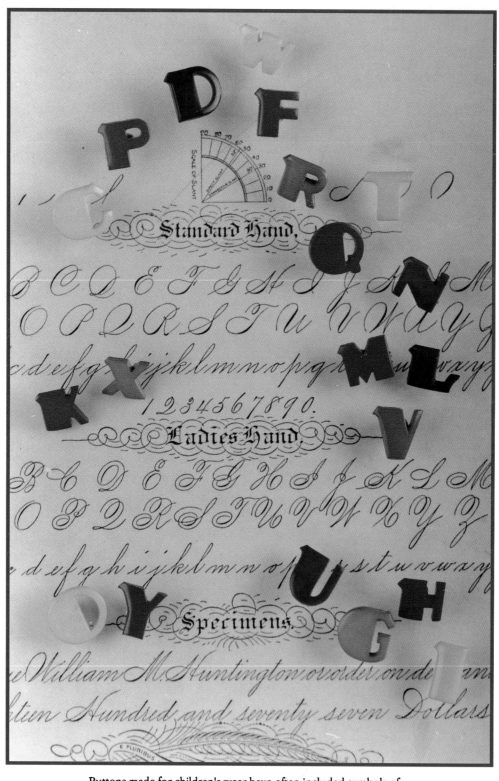

Buttons made for children's wear have often included symbols of schooling. These are from one of the many sets of realistic alphabet buttons that have been manufactured in the last fifty years.

A rare set of carved vegetable-ivory buttons from the 1930s.

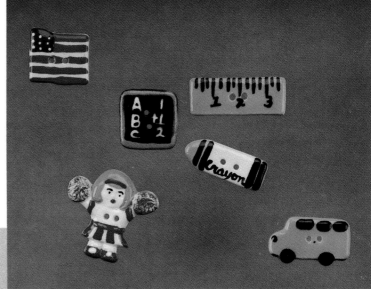

Glazed ceramic, realistic, sew-through buttons, ca. 1980s.

Some of the various school-themed buttons that have been produced include the rare, chunky Lucite letters in the center, brass, Bakelite, celluloid, glass, plastic, and fabric (the apple for the teacher). They range from the 1930s to 1980.

Then they took a Holiday.

Antique buttons with holiday themes are quite unusual. The top
brass button has a silver escutcheon of St. Nicholas (Santa). Below
it, Christmas bells pictured on a Victorian, tinted brass button.

Modern Christmas buttons from the 1930s to 1980s, including
painted wood, ceramics, plastics, enameled metal, cast pewter, and
paper covered.

Halloween is not a common theme on buttons. The pumpkin, at left, and the witch are hard plastic; the jack-o-lantern is painted wood. The witch is a rare realistic from the 1930s; the others are ca. 1980.

These Thanksgiving buttons are by Idabelle Byers, a very talented ceramist from Indiana who sells to the public through craft shows more than to button collectors.

Easter bunnies, chicks, and a decorated egg button, from the 80s. Many of the myriad of buttons featuring bunnies and chicks are not particularly hard to find; this would make a good specialization category for a new collector.

Baby on a printed fabric button, ca 1940s.

Little girls; glass realistics from the 1930s.

Plastic kid's faces, buttons from Japan, 1993.

Transfer designs on plastic buttons for children's wear, a type known in the trade as 'kiddie buttons', ca. 1970s-1980s.

Children on pressed and painted wooden buttons, probably from Italy and Czechoslovakia, 1940s-1950s.

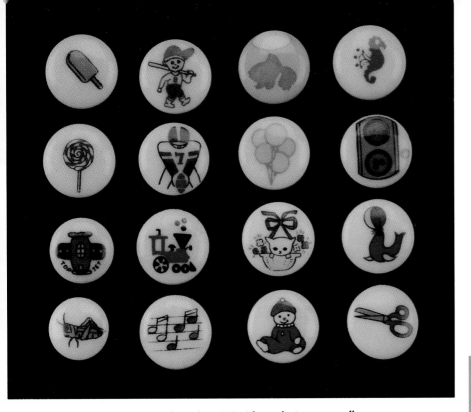

More plastic 'kiddie buttons' from the 1980s. These designs were all from JHB International.

MOTHER GOOSE

Mother Goose stories have long been an inspiration to button designers: these include a transfer-on-plastic Humpty Dumpty at the top from the 1980s, a Bakelite set of realistics from the 1940s at left, and on the card, an unusual set of celluloid buttons from the late 1920s.

A hard-to-complete set of enameled brass Mother Goose
story-inspired buttons 'popping' out of the pages of a book, ca.
1950s.

Ceramic buttons with transfer designs of eight of the most beloved
Mother Goose tales. These sets, with four buttons apiece, were
made in Japan for American button dealer Lois Calkins in the early
1950s.

CHILDRENS' LITERATURE

Little Boy Blue, in two versions from the nineteenth century. Left, black glass with painted incised design, and right, molded brass.

Raggedy Ann and Andy, plastic transfer-decorated button, ca. 1980s.

The characters found in Beatrix Potter's stories of Peter Rabbit are among the most beloved in all of children's literature. The button at the top is dyed vegetgable ivory from the 1920s, part of a very rare set. Directly below it, an enameled brass Peter Rabbit button from the 1980s. The other buttons with transfer designed on plastic , of Hunca Munca, Peter Rabbit, Squirrel Nutkinn, and so on, we were also sold in the 1980s.

Two-dimensional pressed-plastic buttons picturing Paddington Bear.

Winnie the Pooh transfered on plastic, ca. 1980s.

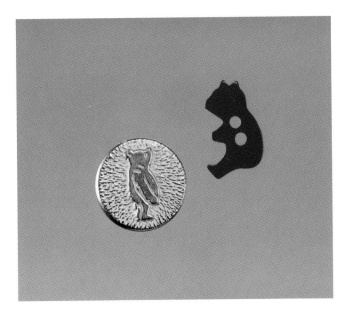

A.A. Milne's beloved Winnie the Pooh is the most famous and beloved Teddy Bear of all. At left, pressed brass, and right, plastic, ca. 1970s.

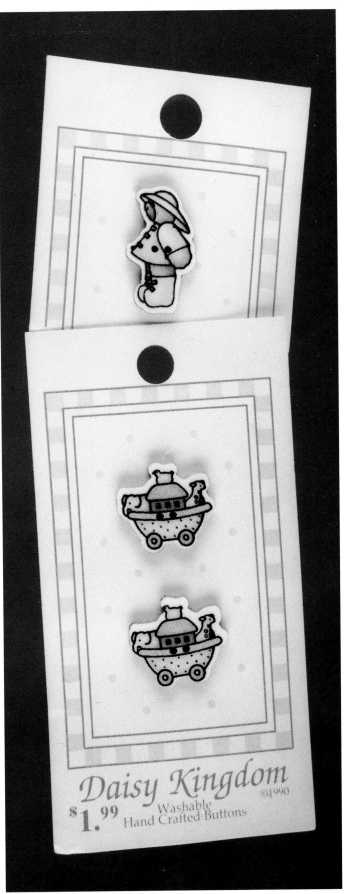

At the top, Paddington Bear, and below, the ark; wooden buttons from the late 1980s.

CARTOON CHARACTERS

Woody Woodpecker, transfer on plastic button, ca. 1980s. *Courtesy of Judy Wehner*

Donald Duck and Mickey Mouse, the two most beloved characters from Walt Disney Studios, are transferred on plastic buttons from France, 1980s. This is one of many types of Disney buttons that have been in production, off and on, in various countries, since the early 1930s.

Buster Brown seen on buttons from the late-nineteenth century, two of brass and, at bottom, a brass escutcheon on steel. Buster's dog, Tige, is pictured with him on the largest button.

Enamel on brass.

The phenomenal success of television's animated-cartoon shows from Hanna Barbera Studios, starting in the 1960s, brought various spin-off products, including these buttons. They are already rare. Huckleberry Hound, Yogi Bear, Quick Draw McGraw, and Elroy Jetson appear as transfer designs on plastic. This is the only known type of button produced with the Hanna Barbera characters on it.

No other comic strip character seems to have found universal love as has Snoopy, from Charles Schultz's *Charlie Brown*. There have been many buttons inspired by this comic strip, but Snoopy outnumbers all the other characters combined in numbers of portrayals. This one is a painted-wood realistic, ca. 1970s.

Snoopy and Woodstock at the piano. A transfer-design on plastic, ca. 1990.

Snoopy in various incarnations! Painted-plastic buttons with the designs molded in relief, ca. late 1980s.

Enameled-brass realistics of Snoopy and Woodstock, ca. 1990.

Transfers on plastic from the 1980s, showing the hapless Charlie Brown, his friend the sharp-tongued Lucy, and Snoopy's bird buddy Woodstock.

TOYS AND PLAYTHINGS

Children were often shown on buttons at play during the nineteenth century; their toys have not been nearly as often featured. These buttons all picture hobbyhorses--only the pressed-tin button (furthest right) and the pressed-brass button (furthest left) are from the nineteenth century. The others are of plastic, pewter, or glass, and date from 1940-1990.

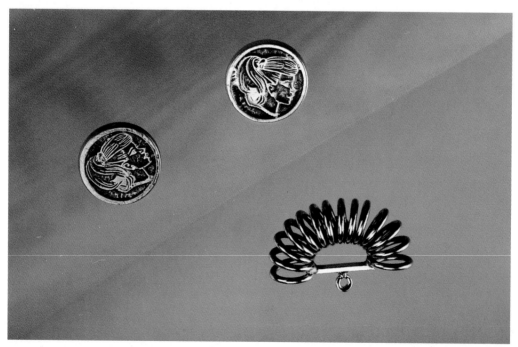

Images of two of the most popular toys of the 1960s are seen here: the Barbie doll and the Slinky toy. The Barbie buttons (there is also a white pearlized nylon one with the same head facing the opposite direction) were not sold as buttons but came sewed on girls' clothing that was produced under the Barbie label for a short time in the early 1960s. They are very rare and very collectible. The Slinky button, from the late 1950s, is even less seldom seen, but is not nearly as sought after by general collectors.

Teddy Bears. Porcelain buttons made for collectors, ca. 1990.

This panda button, a transfer on plastic, was made during the excitement surrounding the arrival at the National Zoo in Washington D.C. of two giant pandas from China following the détente between the two countries, after many years of estrangement, early in the 1970s.

Teddy Bear buttons made from the 1930s through the 1980s of glass, ceramic, plastic, and pewter.

CRITTERS AND ANIMALS
CATS

A rare type of button from last years of the 1800s, the cat is lithographed directly on metal and set in brass.

Painted-ceramic button from artist Janice Young who does many custom buttons for collectors, ca. 1990.

An extremely rare, very large Bakelite realistic cat button from the 1930s. It has three shanks on back to help steady it on fabrics, a metal nose, and inlaid rhinestone eyebrows. The mouse is a brass realistic with tiny black glass eyes, ca. 1960s.

The kitty and the lizard, from the fable by Fontaine. A wonderfully
designed, pierced-brass button from the nineteenth century.

Cats. Brass and tin picture buttons from the late-nineteenth century.

Cat's head, handmade of Fimo clay, commercially available in 1992-93. *Courtesy of Blue Moon Button Art.*

Cat of Fimo clay, ca. 1991-1993. *Courtesy of Blue Moon Button Art.*

Realistic cats, in plastic, enameled brass, sterling silver, silver-plated copper, Arita porcelain (from Japan), pewter, brass, and glazed ceramic, ca. 1930s-1990.

Twentieth-century cat buttons. Top row: incised plastic, glass paperweight by Theresa Rarig (1950s), and cast-pewter copy of an antique button design. Center row: aluminum cat playing with a mouse, transfer on ceramic, molded jasper ware, and pewter. Bottom, pewter, lithograph on metal, Satsuma pottery (Japan, 1950s), porcelain, and enameled brass.

DOGS

Dog buttons from three centuries, in every breed imaginable, are a popular collectors' specialty. Such buttons run the gamut from those made for wear on men's sporting and hunting jackets of the 1700s and 1800s, to women's and children's buttons of the 1900s, with designs ranging from elegant to silly. Those pictured here are from the 1800s and include two of black glass at left (one with a red-lustre finish)--one with a hunter and his dog, and the other of a little girl hugging her huge Newfoundland--a pierced brass button with a dog chained in a doghouse, and a lovely carved pearl cameo set in an engraved wooden base.

Dog carrying a basket by the handle, ca. 1880s.

Whippets. Brass hunting-coat buttons, silver-lustred black-glass dress button and a brass waistcoat button with molded-glass center, ca. mid-1800s.

Basset hound plunging through a paper hoop, silver-plated brass, ca. 1870s-1870.

St. Bernard (smooth coated). Steel with molded-brass center, ca. mid-1800s.

English setter. Extremely rare button made of block tin, beautifully engraved, ca. 1780-1820.

Retrievers. Iridescent-lustred molded black-blass, and pressed brass, ca. late 1800s.

Harriers. Hunting-jacket buttons: two of brass, mid-1800s, and one engraved silver, 1700s.

Greyhounds. Left, vegetable ivory with brass escutcheon; center, pressed aluminum; right, pressed brass. Left and center were for hunt clothes, ca. mid-to-late 1800s.

Bloodhounds. Hunting-jacket buttons: brass with cast-iron center (a rare material for this use) and die-stamped brass, ca. mid-1800s.

Borzoi. Tortoiseshell inlaid with silver and tesserae (chips of pearl), ca. 1860s-1880s.

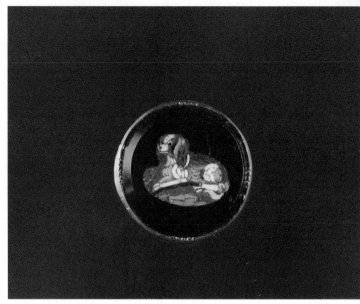

King Charles Spaniel. Man's waistcoat button, brass with micro-mosaic black glass center, ca. 1850s-1880s.

Cocker Spaniel. Pressed and engraved brass, ca. 1800s.

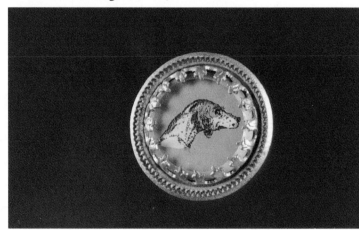

Foxhound. Rare eglomisé (reverse painting on glass) centered brass waistcoat button, ca. 1800s.

Boxers. Brass, pewter, and mother-of-pearl, ca. early 1900s.

Dandie Dinmont Terrier. Pressed brass, ca. late 1800s.

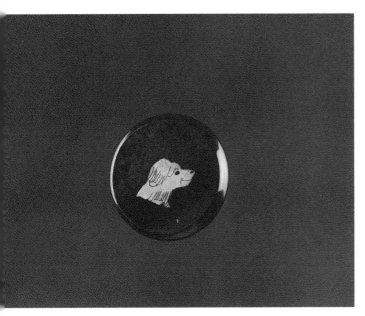

Kuvasz. Acid-etched design on black glass.

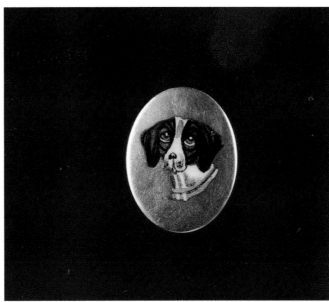

Appenzell. Emaux-peint (painted enamel) on sterling, ca. early 1900s.

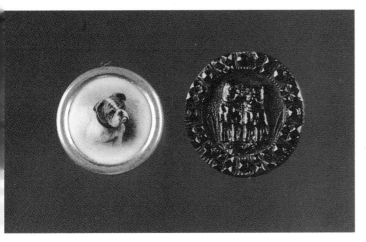

Miniature Boston Terriers. A lithograph set in brass on a waistcoat button, and molded black-glass, late 1800s.

Pekingese. Molded black glass with partial gold-lustre finish, ca. mid-to-late 1800s.

English Springer Spaniel. Stamped and hand-chased brass head within a diamond-cut steel border trimmed with faceted cut-steel rivets.

Clumber Spaniels. Lower left, mid-nineteenth century molded black dyed horn. The late-nineteenth century stamped-brass and the early-twentieth century celluloid were made with the same die pattern.

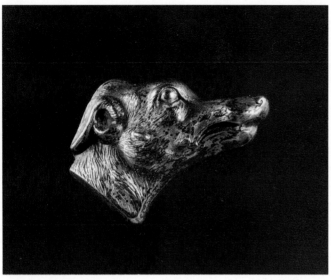

Pharoah Hound. Brass realistic, early 1900s.

West Highland Terrier. Brass realistic, 1940s-1950s.

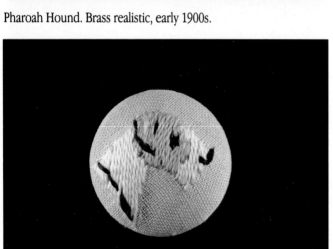

Airedale Terrier. Embroidered linen, ca. 1920s-1930s.

Staffordshire Bull Terrier. Pierced vegetable ivory with intaglio glass center rimmed in brass, ca. 1900-1920.

Bulldog. Molded and painted wood-pulp realistic, ca. late 1920s-1930s.

German Shepherd. Celluloid realistic, 1930s.

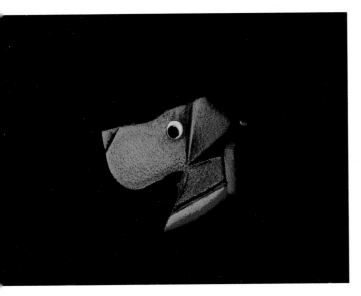

Irish Terrier. Leather realistic, stamped and painted, marked 'France' on reverse. A designer's button, ca. 1930s.

Sussex Spaniel. Molded plastic, ca. 1940s-1950.

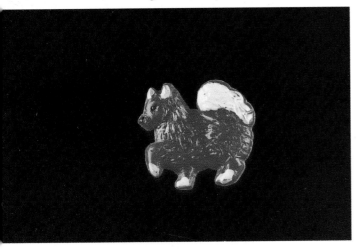

Spitz. Paint-trimmed plastic, ca. 1940s.

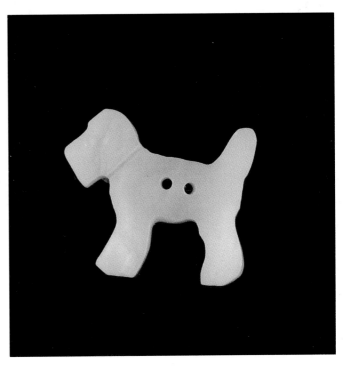

Welsh Terrier. Mother-of-pearl realistic, ca. 1930s.

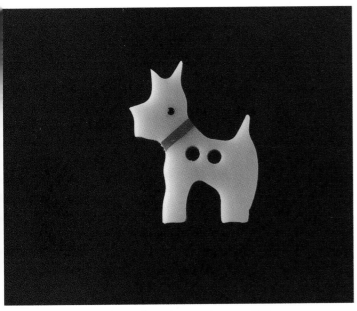

Fox Terrier. Bakelite with Art-Deco styling, ca. 1930s.

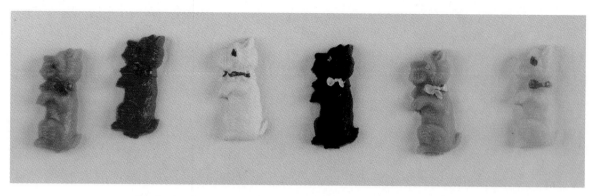

No dog has been pictured on as many buttons as the Scotch Terrier, although they date almost exclusively to the early-twentieth century. This is a set of paint-trimmed plastic realistics, ca. 1930s.

Scotties. Celluloid with brass inlay, painted wood, reflective two-piece glass, Bakelite, celluloid wafer with hollow-molded celluloid trim, molded wood pulp (Syrocco or Burwood), ca. 1920s-1930s.

Poodles. Celluloid, 1920s; electro-plated plastic; and Satsuma pottery, 1950s.

Labrador Retriever. Engraved and pigmented. Polysester set in brass. Blazer button, ca. 1990.

Miniature Schnauzer. Satsuma pottery, ca. 1950s.

Pointers. Reverse painted, molded-glass intaglio set in brass, ca. mid-1900s.

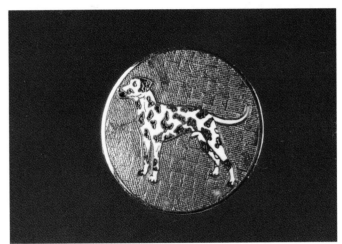

Dalmatian. Enamel on silver-colored metal, ca. 1980s.

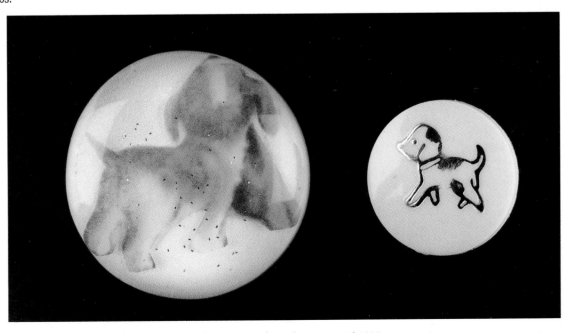

Beagle puppies. Plastic buttons, mid-1900s.

HORSING AROUND

Known in the United States by the trade names Burwood and Syrocco, buttons such as this were made from a molded and painted wood pulp composition in the late 1920s and the 1930s.

Modern buttons (1930s to 1970s) featuring horses' heads, including celluloid, pewter, glass, brass, enameled brass, aluminum, and plastic.

Nineteenth-century buttons with horses' heads including molded and silvered black-glass at left, and three of molded brass. The center button is a colored lithograph mounted as a gold-rimmed waistcoat (man's vest) button, ca. 1895-1910.

GOING BATTY

This wonderfully detailed bat button was made in France, ca. 1989.

Hard-plastic realistic bat from Japan, ca. 1993.

Late-nineteenth-century brass button with a buffalo head.

BEAR MARKET, BULL MARKET

Bakelite, wood, plaster, aluminum, and copper buttons with bears
and bulls. Except for the aluminum bull (late 1800s), they date from
the 1930-1950s period.

TURTLES AND FROGS

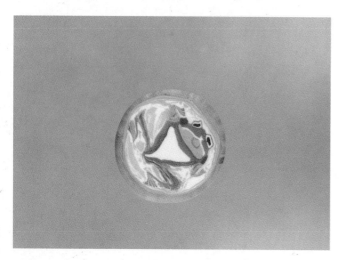

Carved-horn frog button from Africa.

Handmade Fimo-clay button with a frog design, ca. 1990s, done in what is known as a tile inlay technique.

This is a tortoise tortoise! A tortoiseshell button inlaid with silver from Mexico, ca. 1945-1950.

Glass button made by artist Julie Clinton of Washington state. The swirled glass base has a cased and overlay-trimmed, lampworked glass turtle on top, with legs of goldstone (adventurine glass).

Colorful and deeply convex, realistic celluloid turtle, ca. 1930s.

Wooden realistic button.

Coconut shell realistic tortoise.

Two birds and a bee! From left, painted wood, enameled brass, and Bakelite, ca. 1930s-1950s.

Left, imitation tortoiseshell realistic made of plastic, and right, a very thick plastic button with hand-painted ducklings, ca. 1940s.

Three different types of horn buttons with bird designs: left, pressure-molded; center, unusual highly-domed shape with brass inlay; right, pressed-horn base with brass escutcheon, ca. mid-nineteenth century.

Owls seem to lend themselves to creative interpretation, and owl-themed buttons from the nineteenth century, such as these three, are many and varied. These are especially nice examples.

Copper button, nineteenth century, with an unusual rooster design.

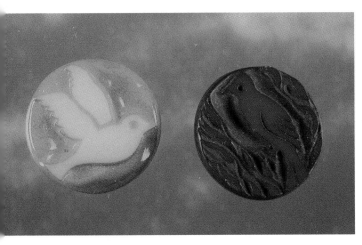

These are very special glass buttons made in West Germany in the 1950s. They were overlaid, or cased, in a second color of glass before the bird designs were hand cut in relief.

Inlaid mother-of-pearl bird, post-1970.

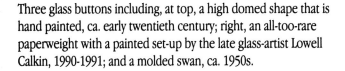

Three glass buttons including, at top, a high domed shape that is hand painted, ca. early twentieth century; right, an all-too-rare paperweight with a painted set-up by the late glass-artist Lowell Calkin, 1990-1991; and a molded swan, ca. 1950s.

An assortment of bird buttons including, upper right, a gold-foil centered paperweight by the late, world-renowned glass-artist Charles Kaziun, ca. 1940s. The lower right penguin is Lucite. At upper left, a transfer on porcelain set in brass from France. Two enameled brass birds, ca. 1980s, are lower left.

Wood realistics.

Plastic set of realistic birds with hand-painted trim, from the 1940s.

Although this parrot 'realistic' appears to be made of metal, it is actually electroplated plastic, ca. 1930s-1940s.

Wonderfully designed and whimsical, each of these features an unusual celluloid bird and dates from the 1930s. The stork at left is a deluxe example, the result of a highly detailed molding process. The handpainted pelican on the right is attached to a wooden button base. The chick is solid molded.

If you can't swim......

..... Duck!

Victorian brass buttons with duck themes. The brass duck at left is centered in a tôle-like painted and etched brass cup; the ducks on the center button are steel.

Man's blazer button of molded brass, ca. 1990, pictured twice its actual size.

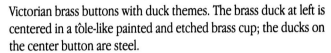

She quacked! Very silly realistic, ca. 1930s-1940s.

Painted-plaster caricature duck from the 1950s.

Hard plastic, paint-trimmed realistics, ca. 1930s.

Large molded-glass button, bee on honeycomb, ca. 1900-1920. This was produced as both a button and a hairpin ornament.

Unusual molded-composition button with a very detailed, plated-metal bee under-glass, ca. 1940s-1950s.

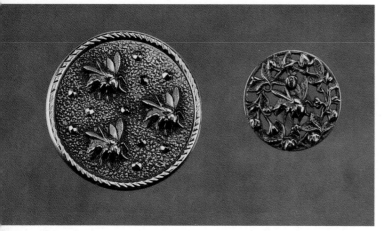

Bees. At left, the molded brass, medallion-like piece was set into a steel base. At right, pierced brass with a bee hovering over strawberry plants.

A silver-plated fly on brass. Who would have wanted to fasten flies all over their clothes? Nevertheless, during the mid-to-late 1900s, there was a great fad for bugs on buttons and many pictured flies.

From the late-nineteenth century, an assortment of insects parade across these buttons: from left, intaglio-molded black-glass beetle, incised black glass, mother-of-pearl with carved waterbug, molded brass, molded iridescent-lustred black glass, same, cast brass silkworm, and a hand-painted silkworm on a horn button.

Modern buttons with insect designs include ceramic, glass, and plastic, ca. 1940-1960.

Lady bugs! The buttons in this group include examples from throughout the twentieth century, in wood, plastic, Bakelite, pearl, celluloid, glass, brass, and vegetable ivory.

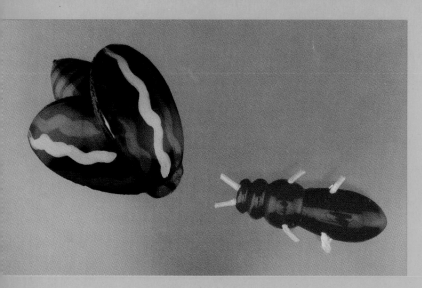

Linoleum button with hand-painted butterfly, from Mexico, 1940s.

Celluloid realistic bugs, ca. 1930s. The red one has white rubber legs and antennae.

Butterflies aloft! Mother-of-pearl, ceramic, glazed porcelain, Bakelite, plastic, plaster, coconut shell, tòle, enameled metal, black glass, wood, and brass butterfly buttons ranging in date from ca. 1880s (black glass) to the 1980s (porcelain monarch).

Left, carved mother-of-pearl cameo attached to the pearl base with steel rivets; right, an inlay of dyed mother-of-pearl on a composition button, ca. late 1800s.

THE FLOWERS AND THE TREES

Painted-enamel pansy on brass, bordered with enamel pierrieres,
this is a deluxe button from the late-nineteenth century.

Assorted nineteenth-century, floral-themed buttons of brass,
pewter, steel, glass (at far right), and (at upper left) carved, shaded
mother-of-pearl.

Handpainted porcelain button set in a brass frame.

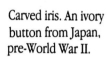

Carved iris. An ivory button from Japan, pre-World War II.

Satsuma painted-pottery button from Japan, ca. 1895-1920s, with cobalt blue background. The thick enamel paint and heavily-gilded detailing differentiate it from more modern examples. Satsumas are snatched up by button and jewelry collectors alike.

Tinted pierced-brass button, late-nineteenth century.

A pierced rose design in hallmarked English silver, ca. 1904.

A rose embroidered on a fabric button.

A daisy, ca. 1880-1890s, in brass with painted background.

The falling leaves of green plastic, orange celluloid, striped glass,
and brass, ca. 1930s-1960s.

More leaves on modern buttons of the 1940s-1960s in brass,
mother-of-pearl, pewter, silver-plate, aluminum, and wood.

From the previous century, these leaf-themed buttons include, in top row: cameo-carved pearl, man's waistcoat button with a foil-designed black-glass paperweight center and molded black-glass with an iridescent gold lustre. In center: pierced brass and etched pearl. In bottom row: pressed aluminum, carved and gilded smoky pearl, brass vest button, and molded black-glass.

For luck, some four-leafed clover buttons in brass, handpainted china, aluminim, steel black glass, and mother-of-pearl. The paperweight button with gold-foil clover in the center was made in the late 1940s by glass-artisan Charles Kazium.

AND THE MOON UP ABOVE

Palm trees in the moonlight, painted on a butterfly wing and set under glass in a silver frame. This technique - also seen in jewelry - was used in the 1920s and 1950s in Africa.

A cut-out fir tree on a pewter button, ca. 1950s.

A lovely, interpretive pierced-brass tree designed in the Art Nouveau style with cut-steel rivets over an iridescent celluloid background and brass base, ca. 1880s-1890s.

A handpainted tropical-beach in moonlight scene on a large wooden button, ca. 1940s.

Palm trees, two of celluloid and one of painted wood, ca. 1930s.

AND A THING CALLED LOVE

Pressed brass button from the 1960s.

Pressed and painted wood buttons featuring kissing couples from Czechoslovakia, 1930s.

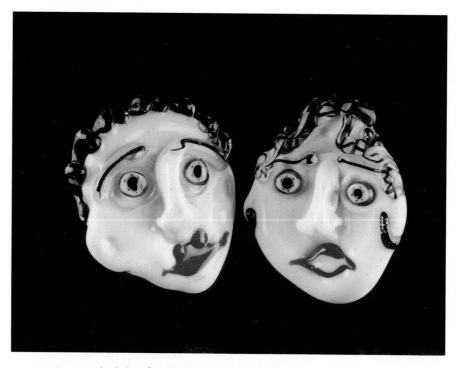

Lampworked glass faces by American artist Julie Clinton, 1992.

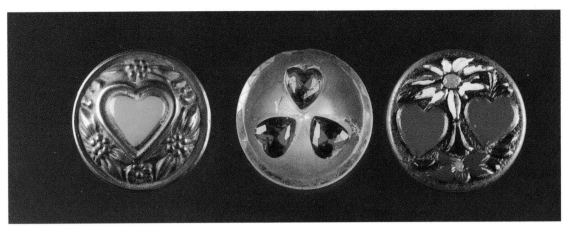

Heart-themed buttons from the 1950s include, from left, painted embossed brass, center, glass inset with faceted glass hearts, and molded pewter with enameled center heart.

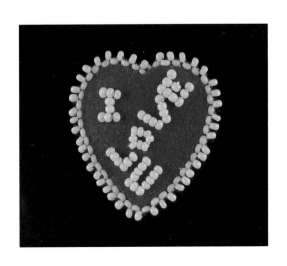

A large and garish, hollow-blown red celluloid heart on a celluloid wafer base, ca. 1920s.

Hearts from after 1950 except for the handpainted china button with a pine cone (ca. 1895-1910). Materials include glass, plastic, wood, ceramic, Fimo clay, molded brass, and aluminum.

A beadwork message written out on a felt button.

FAIRIES AND FANTASIES

A fairy as a pierced brass button, ca. 1890-1920.

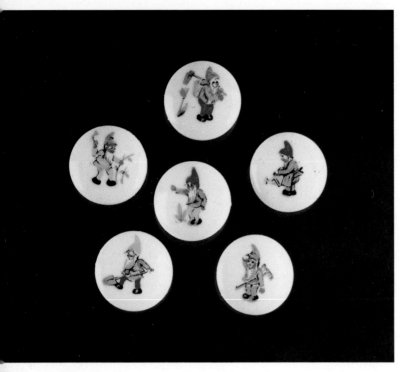

Adorable gnomes in transfers on plastic buttons.

Fairies on nineteenth-century buttons made of pressed tin, brass, dyed brass, and engraved vegetable ivory.

Pegasus, the flying horse of various mythologies worldwide, as it has been interpreted by button designers. The buttons pictured are made of enameled metal, brass, steel, copper, pewter, silver-plate, Arita porcelain and Satsuma pottery (both Japanese), painted wood (France), leather, glass, silver-lustred black glass, and mother-of-pearl. Ca. 1880-1980.

Unicorns were not often used as a theme by button designers, but a few can be found. These examples include printed fabric, enameled copper, glass paperweights, pressed brass, and plastic buttons. They range in date from the 1890s to the 1990s.

FRUITS, NUTS, AND VEGGIES

Fruit realistics from the 1930s to the 1950s made of celluloid, wood and plastics.

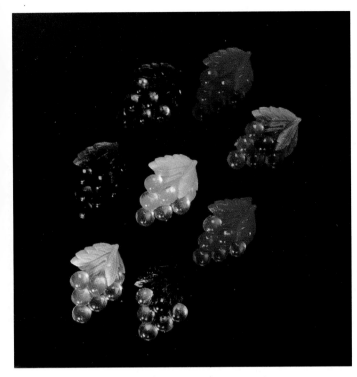

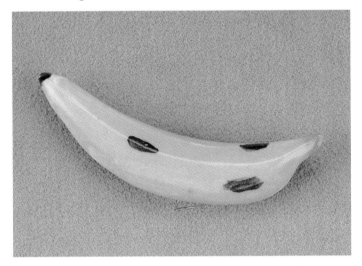

Glass fruit-shaped realistics were made during the middle of the nineteenth century and again in the 1930s. These are the earlier types, with the exception of the orange at lower left.

A set of celluloid grape realistics from the 1930s. The grapes are hollow and glow from within because of a reflective finish inside.

This large, painted-ceramic banana has a metal-loop shank inserted in the back.

A large and hollow celluloid realistic apple with a chain hanging from the shank, for use on an overcoat, ca. 1940.

Painted-plaster fruit buttons from the 1940s.

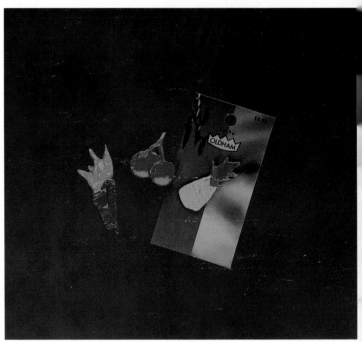

American high-fashion designer Todd Oldham began to produce a line of buttons, mostly in metal with whimsical themes, early in the 1990s in conjunction with Streamline Buttons. These enameled realistics are but a few of the selections offered in his 1992 "fruits & vegetables" line.

Set of paint-trimmed, plastic realistics as different vegetables, from the 1940s.

Celluloid vegetables at left, and at right, painted-wood ones, ca. 1930s.

Oh, Nuts!

Many different nut-shaped buttons have been produced. All of these are acorns, and although most are mid-twentieth-century examples, the three smallest (at the top and just below) are from the mid-nineteenth century. Top row from left: molded black-glass, brass waistcoat button with glass acorn attached, and carved wood. Center arched row: aluminum, carved wood, antler with sterling acorn, cameo-carved pearl, wood, and gilded celluloid. Center row: celluloid wafer with attached celluloid acorn, painted Bakelite, and carved wood. Bottom row: plastic, molded brass, plastic with celluloid trim, and celluloid.

VEHICLES

Bicyclers from the 1930s appear as a painted, pressed wood button at left and in a glass intaglio set in brass and mounted on a leather button. Both of these buttons are Czech.

The automobile has been featured on buttons since its invention. Early buttons picturing automobiles were worn on "duster coats"; two of the buttons in the second row were duster buttons from the 1900 era--the molded horn at center and the pressed brass at right. The others here date between 1930 and the 1980s. The top button is a finely designed wooden realistic button from Spain where automobile racing is taken very seriously.

These work-clothes buttons picturing railroad trains date from
1915-1940.

Perhaps designed to represent the ocean liner *Queen Mary*, this is a
Bakelite realistic from the 1930s.

A linoleum button with a hand-painted gondola scene, made in
Mexico in the 1950s.

SPORTS AND GAMES

Oh, come on. Be a Sport about this!

Horseracing is intense sport at many levels. This is a Bakelite button with a molded-brass center from the late 1920s-1930s.

A tiny sampling of the many sport-themed buttons available, these include table tennis, fishing, discus-throwing, golf, soccer, polo, and juggling. The brass fisherman is from the nineteenth century and the rest are from the twentieth.

Two Bakelite buttons from the early 1930s. A dumbell at the left and a very funny (and rare) weight lifter dressed in leopard skins--probably representing a circus strongman.

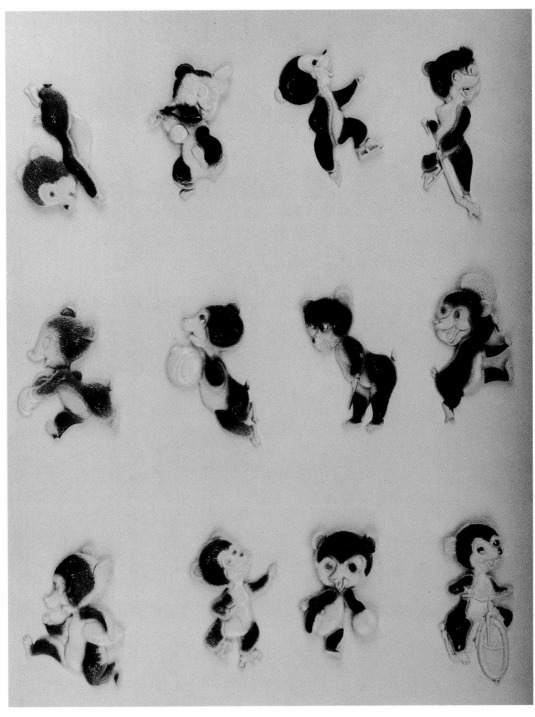

A very unusual set of plastic realistic buttons, from the 1950s. These are the Sugar Crisp© bears, from the cereal of the same name, engaged in various sports: diving, baseball, ice-skating, ice-hockey, boxing, basketball, golfing, tennis, football, roller-skating, volley-ball, and bicycling. Never sold, they were premiums for the company, available one-by-one with boxtops. Courtesy of Colleen Farevaag.

Close-up of one of the Sugar Crisp Bear buttons, and the back of another showing the molded markings.

Are you Game to try collecting yet?

Sporting equipment on buttons. Many examples of sport-themed buttons date from the nineteenth century, yet those shown here date range from the 1920s to 1990. The largest football shown, and the golf bag are celluloid buttons from the 1930s. The realistic sterling-silver squash racquet is a decade older. The two most unusual buttons shown are the realistic badminton shuttlecock made of Bakelite and cork, and the round grey plastic button picturing a curling stone. The remaining are buttons of wood, aluminum, plaster, leather, porcelain, plastic, pewter, and mother-of-pearl.

The Chinese game mah-jongg was extraordinarily popular in the United States in the 1900-1930s period. At left, a carved vegetable-ivory button engraved with a mah-jongg tile, and at right, an engraved Bakelite realistic tile.

A set of six realistic dominos buttons and a set of painted mah-jongg tile-shaped buttons, ca. 1930s.

Playing games, with buttons! Top row: chess board of electro-plated plastic. Center row: lithograph of playing cards on celluloid base under a clear celluloid cover, the four-card suit insignia transfered on porcelain set in brass, and a bingo card of Bakelite. Bottom row, celluloid tic-tac-toe game and one of electro-plated plastic, an engraved plastic Scrabble© tile, two black glazed-pottery dice buttons and one die of red Bakelite. All date ca. 1930-1950s.

The End. or is there no End?!

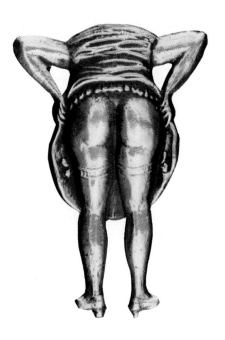

Sterling-silver button marked "Souvenir of Paris" on the reverse.
Actual size, 1 2/3 ".

SUGGESTED READING

The following publications are recommended for a variety of views on buttons and collecting:

About Buttons by Peggy Ann Osborne, Schiffer Publishing Ltd., Atglen, PA, 1994. A milestone in the field, this unique book is a cultural history and an art reference illustrated with nearly 1200 photographs showing buttons to be no less than actual reflections of the world around them. Unprecedented in its approach, it focuses on the original intent behind the designs of buttons, from the most elegant 18th-century examples through the buttons of the 1990s. Full color, with a guide to values included.

The Big Book of Buttons by Elizabeth Hughes and Marion Lester, reprinted by New Leaf Publishers, Sedgwick, ME, 1991. Overwhelming to a non-collector but indispensable to a serious one, this includes thousands of buttons by name and subject (mostly shown in black and white photographs) and has long been the definitive book for active collector/competitors. Contains pricing information.

Button, Button by Peggy Ann Osborne, Schiffer Publishing Ltd., Atglen, PA, 1993. A useful tool for collectors at all levels, this is an in-depth identification guide to button materials, age, and construction. Full color with a guide to prices included.

The Button Lover's Book by Marilyn V. Green, Chilton Book Co., Radnor, PA, 1991. Geared strictly towards the newcomer and crafts people, this cheerful book is nevertheless laden with practical advice and information, including the most extensive listing of retail dealers, sources, and suppliers in print.

Buttons by Diana Epstein and Millicent Safro, Harry Abrams, New York. Perhaps the most beautiful button book ever published, it gives readers a glimpse of the world's most elegant button collection while its erudite and informative text explains the art involved. No price suggestions. Full color.

The Collector's Encyclopedia of Buttons by Sally Luscomb, Crown Publishers, Inc., New York, NY 1967. Reprinted by Schiffer Publishing Ltd., Atglen, PA, 1993. A classic reference, the best available for information on manufacturing techniques and manufacturers (mostly American). No collector should be without this book. Most photographs in black and white, without any current pricing information.

The Colorful World of Buttons by Vivian Beck Ertell, The Pyne Press, Princeton, NJ, 1973. Another beautiful book showcasing one of the best private collections of 18th-century buttons ever gathered. No pricing information. Full color.

The Complete Button Book by Lillian Smith Albert and Kathryn Kent, Doubleday, Garden City, NY, 1949. No longer a standard because of the small photos and years-ago publication, this nevertheless remains one of my favorites, covering a wide spectrum of buttons by material and subject. No pricing information. Black and white.

Record of American Uniform and Historical Buttons, by Alphaeus (Dewey) Albert, Boyertown Publishing Co., Boyertown, PA, Revised ed., 1976. The standard reference in the field, now out of print. Though outdated, this is still an essential reference for a military or political collector. Pricing suggestions too old to be of value except to compare relative scarcity.

Transportation Uniform Buttons, *Volume I-Railroads*, 1991, *Volume II-Transit*, 1993, by Donald VanCourt, Madison, NJ, privately published. Over 2,000 transportation-lines uniform buttons from the United States and Canada, illustrated and described.

The National Button Bulletin, National Button Society. Past issues and present. Back issues are often available for purchase at button shows, from dealers (see Societies.).

Just Buttons Magazine, printed from 1938 to 1979. This slick little magazine was a joy, laden with information. Back issues can sometimes be found through button dealers.

BUTTON SOCIETIES

The National Button Society. Membership includes The National Button Bulletin, 5 issues annually. For information about membership, write to Lois Pool, National Sec'y, 2733 Juno Place, Akron, OH 44313.

State Clubs throughout the United States: contact the National Button Society for a list. Most of them also publish bulletins or newsletters for their members.

The British Button Society. Membership includes the quarterly Button Lines. For information write c/o M. Jones, 27 Pitch & Pay Park, Sneyd Park, Bristol B59 INL, England.

The Button Collector Society of Australia. P.O. Box 565, Magil, South Australia, 5072, Australia.

In addition, there are dealers specializing in buttons in the United States, England, France, the Netherlands, Japan, Germany, Belgium, Scotland, Wales, Switzerland, the Philippines, and Canada, and serious collectors worldwide.

GUIDE TO VALUES

The following guide is intended only as a point of reference for new collectors to enable them to judge the relative desirability or rarity of the various types of buttons. It is in no way intended as a price list. The ranges are based on an average of what I think specialized dealers would charge. Positions are indicated by the letter codes:
L = left, R = right, C = center, T = top, B = bottom.

PAGE	POSITION	US DOLLARS
Title Page	T	1
	CL	1
	CR	3-5
	B	.25
Acknowledgments		5
Dedication		2
Foreword		10-15
Introduction		5
8		1-10
	Pinna shell	50-75
9	Laminated	1-15
	B	15-20
10	TL	3-15
10	BR	4-30
11		25-30
	Set of 10	300-350
12	T	6-25
12	B	6-25
13	Corner buttons	2-4
13	C	1-8
14		1-9
15	TL	1-2
15	TR	2-12
15	BL	1-4
15	BR	3-11
16	TL	12-18
16	CR	6-8
16	B	9-15
17	TR	12-18
17	C	8-12
17	CR	22-28
17	L	25-25
17	BR	4-7
18	T	10-15
18	B	8-12
19		2-20
20	T	25-35
20	B	1-23
21	T	8-12
21	B	3-15
22		1-7
23	T	.50-6
23	BL	5
23	BR	2-4
24	TL	20-25
24	BR	1-4
25	TL	15-18 card
25	TR	2-5
25	B	2-8
26	TL	2-3
26	TR	5-7
26	B	1-10
27	TL Mermaid	1-15
27	CR	4-7
27	BL	2-7
27	BR	2-3
28		3-15
29	Large enamels	3-25
30	T	5-25
30	B	3-7
31		2-22
32	T	2-10
32	B	4-8
33	TL	3-4
33	C	4-7
33	B	4-7
	Danforth	1-2
34	TL	10-14
34	TR	10-12
34	CL	3-5
34	BR set of 10	40-50
35	TL	20-25 ea.
35	TR	24-30
35	B	4-7
36	TL	2-8
36	BR	5-9
37	T	5-7
37	B	2-18
38	TL	2-4
38	CR	3-10
38	BL	2-13
39		4 (small)-12
40		1-7
41	T	2-5
41	B	6-9
42	L	3-8
42	TR	30-35
42	RC	20-30
42	C	20-25
42	Fly	75-80
42	Spider	85-100
43		3-8
44	T	3-30
44	B	3-8
45	T	1-4
46	Lady's head	2-22
47	TR	25-30
47	C	2-5
47	BR	2-6
48	T	15-25
48	B	50-65
49	TL	25-35
49	TR	35-45
49	BL	20-25
49	BR	20-25
51		.75-3
52	TL	2-4
52	R	5-8
52	BL	2-5
53	T	4-22
53	B	2-3
54	T	1-30
55	TR	22-25
55	B	7-18
56		3-25
57	TR	30-45
57	C	25-35
57	BL	30-45
57	Others	5-10
58	T	5-6
58	B	
59		4-12
60	T	20-28
60	B	7-20
61	T (bottom & top right)	2-25
61	B	3-4
62		1-12
63		2-9
64	TL	2-3
64	TR	5-7
64	BL	3-5
64	BR	1
65	T	4-8
65	B	2-4
66	TL	3-4
66	CR	8-10
66	BR	14-20
67		2-10
68	TL	20-22
68	Others	1-5
69	T	2-5
69	B	4-7
70	T	50-5
70	C & B	2-4
70	BR	5-15
71	TR (scarce)	75-90 set
71	CL	6-10
71	BR	5-6
72	TL	3-7
72	C (rare)	10-12 ea.
72	B	3-4
73	TL (rare)	60-65 set
73	TR (rare)	45-60 set
73	BR (rare)	60-65 set

73	TR (rare)	45-60 set		93	T	2-3		109	CR	20-22
73	BR (rare)	8-10 ea		93	CL	2		109	B (Aluminum)	3-30
74	TL	2 Set		93	CR	2		110		3-12
74	TR	5-8		93	BL	2-3		111	T	2-3
74	CL	2-3		93	BR	1.50-2		111	B	6-15
74	CR	2-3		94	T	.50-3		112	T	10-30
74	BL	40-45		94	B	20-25		112	C	12-25
74	BR	7-9			Barbie	5-6		112	BL	30-40
	L	2-3		95	TL	4-8		113	TL	6-10
75	TL	4-5		95	TR	2-3		113	TR	4-8
75	CR	8-12		95	B	1-7		113	CR	7-55
75	BL	14-16		96	TL	20-25			(Calkin Paperweight)	
76	TL	2-3		96	TR	4-6		113	B	3-12
76	TR	8-15		96	B	75-85			Kaziun pw	100-125
76	CL	.50-2			Cat	1-2		114	TL	18-20 set
76	BR	2-3		97	T	25-35		114	TR	2-3
76	BL	3-4		97	B	5-25		114	CR	2-4
77	T	35-45 set		98	TL & TR	4		114	BL	5-25
77	CL	35-45		98	B (Arita)	2-75		115	TR	9-20
77	CR	2-3		99	T (Satsuma)	2-50		115	Others	5
77	BL	2-4		99	BL	5-20		116	TL	18-20
77	BR	4-6		99	BR	5-7		116	TR	8-12
78	TL	7-15		100	T	10-12		116	CL	7-15
78	TR	15-20		100	CL	12-15		116	CR	5-10
78	CR	1-2		100	CR	18-24		116	B	4-10
78	BL	7-10		100	BL	Too rare to price		117	T	1-4
79	TL	5-7						117	B	1-3
79	TR	5-6		100	BR	5-9		118	TL	4-6
79	CL	4-5		101	T	10-30		118	CL	5-7
79	BR	6-8		101	C	5-18		118	CR	5-9
79	BL	25-30		101	B	10-18		118	B	2-12
80		2-21		102	TL	25-35		119	T	25-35
81	T	2-20		102	TR	40-55		119	B	4-12
81	B	2-20		102	CL	5-8		120	TL	12-14
82		.50-1		102	CR	20-35		120	TR	55-75
83	TL	40-45 set		102	BL	3-6		120	CL	12-16
83	CR	2-3		102	BR	5-8		120	CR	30-45
83	B	1-3		103	TL	6-7		120	BL	8-12
84	TL	35-50		103	TR	8-13		120	BR	8-14
	St Nick	10-15		103	CL	5-25		120	B	5-8
84	B	1-4		103	CR	3-6		121	T	2-4
85	TL	1-4		103	BL	5-7		121	B	2-5
85	C	3-5		103	BR	3-10 (horn)		122	T	3-12
85	B	1-4		104	TL	3-5		122	B	1-6
86	TL	3-4		104	TR	3-5			China	10-12
86	TR	2-3		104	CL	8-14			Kaziun pw	30-40
86	CL	1-2		104	CR	15-18		123	TL	8-12
86	CR	2-3		104	BL	22-25		123	TR	5-8
86	B	.50-1.50		104	BR	6-8		123	CL	15-20
87	T	.50-1.50		105	TL	25-30		123	CR	15-18
87	B	15-18		105	TR	2-3		123	B	3-6
	Sets (left & carded) .5			105	CL	2-3		124	TL	2-3
88		3-5		105	BL	6-9		124	C	5-6
89		15-22 ea. set		105	BR	5-7		124	BL	15-20
90	TL	4-8		106	T	10-15 set		125	T	2-3
90	CR	1-1.50		106	C	2-10		125	CL	1-6
90	B	1-5		106	B (Satsuma)	2-55			China	8-12
91	TL	1-2		107	TL	4-6		125	CR	5-7
91	CL	1		107	TR	35-45		125	B	3
91	R	1-1.50		107	CL	12-14		126	TR	8-12
91	BL	1-1.50		107	CR	5-6		126	CL	10-12 set
92	TL	5-7		107	B	2-7		126	BR	5-18
92	TR	4-20		108	TR	20-22		127	T	5-50 (Arita)
92	CR	15-20		108	CL	2-6		127	B	1.50-6
92	BL	5-7		108	BR (Lithograph)	7-30		128		1-7
92	BR	6-10		109	TL	4		129	TL	25-34
				109	TR	4-7			Set of 8	

129	TR	5-7
129	CL	4-6
129	CR	5-8
129	BL	2
130	L	12 set
130	R	5
130	B	5-6
131	Bakelite	1-35
132	T	8-10
132	B	2-25 (horn)
133	T	2-4
133	CR	4-6
133	BL	8-10
134	TR	18-24
134	C	2-8
134	BR	3-22
135		Very rare
136		1-5
137	TR	3-4
137	CL	10 per set
137	BR	1-5
138		15-20
143		10-15 set

A set of very silly buttons made from plastic with painted cork heads, ca. 1940s.

INDEX